have a
glass

A Modern Guide to Wine

have a
glass

Kenji Hodgson | James Nevison

whitecap

For our mothers

Edited by Marial Shea
Proofread by Lesley Cameron
Cover illustration by Henriett Kuti
Cover type design by Roberta Batchelor
Interior design and illustrations by Jacqui Thomas
Interior photographs by Kenji Hodgson and James Nevison

Printed and bound in Canada

National Library of Canada Cataloguing in Publication Data
Nevison, James
    Have a glass: a modern guide to wine / James Nevison and Kenji Hodgson.

Includes index.
ISBN 1-55285-470-1

    1. Wine and wine making. I. Hodgson, Kenji. II. Title.
TP548.N48 2003   641.2'2   C2003-911233-0

The publisher acknowledges the support of the Canada Council for
the Arts and the Cultural Services Branch of the Government of British
Columbia for our publishing program. We acknowledge the financial
support of the Government of Canada through the Book Publishing
Industry Development Program for our publishing activities.

contents

a toast to the good life

It's Friday night, winter 2000, and my friend James Nevison phones me with an impromptu dinner invitation. When I arrive at the apartment, his roommate, Kenji Hodgson, is just shaking off the cold from getting in after his last class of the day. The three of us sit around the kitchen/living room table, talking about the prospects of being newly graduated and/or nearly graduated. Life *after* university—the supposed Promised Land.

James gets up to open a bottle of wine. They are quizzing me on where an English Literature degree will lead a girl these days; I jokingly respond, *Alcoholism, or some variation thereof.* In all seriousness, I turn the question back on each of them: *Now that you have the space to do something, what is it you're planning?*

It's an old question, somewhat unfair and I know it. James and I have been good friends for a few years, and I've known Kenji for almost as long. The same conversation in different contexts. We know the answers change every few months. This time, though, the two housemates seem to have the same glimmer in their eyes. They both smile into their wineglasses, each taking a big sip. Kenji looks up at James, who looks up at me.

"We're thinking of starting a business," James tells me. They have their thoughts on wine, they explain, but more importantly, on matters of style, matters of taste. The idea came out of discussions not unlike the ones we had been having for awhile now, over numerous dinners, coffees, and cocktails: *What constitutes a good life?* We could all agree, and not entirely facetiously, that wine was a part of the answer.

They tell me they are thinking of calling the company *HALFAGLASS*, in honour of the perpetual question. Like everything else at this time in our lives, we can only guess what will come of it. But the topic puts the three of us in good spirits. We sit down to dinner, talking excitedly about their plans for *HALFAGLASS*. Kenji dishes up an excellent green curry and the topic veers towards what kind of wine would best compliment the flavours of the dish. Another bottle of wine is uncorked—and the good spirits flow all night.

———

Another Friday night in winter, two years later. James phones and asks me if I can spare an hour for a drink. We are neighbours at this point. By some strange turn of events, about six jobs, five apartment changes (one of which involved Kenji living in my place for two months while I was travelling) and eight plane rides later, the two of us end up living two blocks away from one another in the same city. James and Kenji have just returned from a two-month trip to Europe, during which time they took part in a *vendage* and started writing a book.

———

A month earlier, a postcard had arrived from France. On the front were three large grape-juice stains and a hand-written inscription: *100% Beaujolais Cru.* The back said:

And so ends the hardest (and yet strangely enjoyable) 8 days of my manual-working life. Resigned to picking grapes in the Burgundy region (Pouilly-Fuissé and Beaujolais to be more precise), I thought I was going to die. The 1st day the back is in agony, by the 3rd the pain spreads to the legs. However, you live with good people (they're crazy, but in a fun way), and by the 5th day the routine sets in. 6 a.m. rise, breakfast.

12 p.m. lunch. 6 p.m. finish. Hey baby, it's the vendage, and it's about as French as you can get. The smashed grapes speak volumes, and respect for the wine grows.

James

The smashed grapes do speak volumes. In the last two years, respect for the wine has certainly grown—both in James and Kenji, as well as amongst the community of family, friends, and colleagues who have watched their vision grow (and who have joined in, sometimes vicariously and sometimes as direct participants, in the requisite schemes, adventures, and, of course, parties that accompanied the development of their educational project). If its goal has been to raise the profile of wine, demystify the esoteric aura of this Old World libation and, in the process, promote the idea of stopping to enjoy a sip of vino in the chase of the good life, *HALFAGLASS* has certainly succeeded in doing so with many of Vancouver's hip twentysomethings. *In case you are wondering, their homebrew is also not bad.*

For many of us in this loose circle of friends, the last two years marked significant, exciting, and vastly different changes—travels around the world and back, new jobs, careers and hobbies, different stages of relationship building, settling in new cities, returns to university, and one or two newborn faces. The question of how to live a good life was always near at hand. *HALFAGLASS*, a testament to hard work, dedicated vision, and a commitment to the good life, continued to be the centre of many of our conversations.

—

When I finally arrive at James's apartment on this November night, he is at his computer, working on the manuscript for *Have a Glass*. We settle in with—*what else?*—a couple of glasses of wine, and he tells me that he and Kenji would be honoured if I would write the foreword to their book. I am, at once, flattered and flabbergasted.

"But I know nothing about wine!" I protest.

James laughs and explains that he and Kenji want someone who knows and understands the *HALFAGLASS* philosophy to write the introduction. They have not asked another "wine expert" because the audience of the book will not necessarily be experts, but more like me—people interested in wine and learning about wine, but above all, interested in the good life. This is the biggest compliment of all.

"Besides," he says "you can't say, after all this, that you don't know anything about wine." I think about my own travels through Europe—my tours through the Bordeaux region, how I finessed my way into a waitressing job with some fast talking about wine, the night I met my boyfriend's family and impressed them with my choice of a fine Australian Shiraz.

As I consider this, I am swirling the liquid around in my glass and watching it slowly pool down to the bottom. "Nice legs," I say. "Quite a bit of oak, but very smooth. Cabernet–Merlot blend?" I ask.

"Bordeaux" James tells me. He raises his glass to me, and I nod, tipping my glass in return.

"Good times," I say to him, and he responds: *Good times.*

Janey Lew

wine
living

chapter one

wine

the good life

This is a book about wine. It is also a book about life. So let's say it's a guide for living with wine. Why wine? Wine is an integral part of a healthy lifestyle, with an uncanny ability to make food taste better, create memorable occasions, and reduce life's disasters to manageable inconveniences. Wine has a storied history and an exciting future, and as you'll see, wine's as simple or as complicated as you make it.

To be honest, it's funny this book even exists. Why devote so many pages to such a simple thing as wine? The answer is, we have a wine complex. Over the years we've surrounded wine with details and irrelevancies that completely detract from its simple enjoyment.

It doesn't have to be this way. Living well does not have to be complicated, even though the good life often seems an elusive construct. Nor does the good life necessarily carry a hefty entrance fee. Break it down into simple components and really you only need good wine, good food, and good company. Yeah, life is a package deal, complete with wayward stresses and tribulations, but put effort and commitment into these three elements and you too can live large.

This book focuses on the "good wine" part of the equation. We hope the following pages show why wine and life pair so nicely.

good

wine,

good

food,

and

good

company

living

the abridged story of wine

Wine has been around since before recorded history. (And therefore hangovers have probably been around since the morning after.) Like all things fermented, it was more than likely an accidental discovery.

ancient wine

Wine first jumps onto the scene with the Egyptians, around 6000 BC, as evidenced from vinous depictions in their

hieroglyphs. Little, however, save fermentation, connects the pharaohs' plonk to the wine you may now have in your cup.

Wine, more or less as we know it, has its roots with the Greeks and Etruscans, circa 1000 BC. Later, the Romans really took vine planting in stride, with wine no doubt important fuel for empire expansion and gala orgies. Following the Greeks' lead, the Romans planted grapevines wherever they colonized, eventually as far north as modern-day Britain. Wine was serious business for Jupiter's followers, as evidenced by the great writer, Pliny the Elder, waxing "in vino sanitas," or, "in wine there is health." It is testament to the Romans' ability and passion that many of modern Europe's finest vineyards were planted at this time.

Of course, we'd be excused if the Romans' libations didn't quite suit our palates. The majority of their wine was made rough and drunk young, commonly mixed with water, spiked with herbs, and served from seven gallon earthenware jugs called *amphorae*. Perhaps the first "party wine," and we use the term loosely.

wine evolves

Wine continued its merry path with little hindrance. In fact, the first miracle of Jesus was turning water into wine (a whopping six amphorae worth) at Cana of Galilee. So with the fall of the Roman Empire, it was the Church that rallied to the winemaking cause. Monasteries were, in no ironic way, the shining lights of the medieval period, antiquated Wal-Mart–like, big-box retailers of skills. They multiplied and magnified in scope, their strict winemaking methods and accounting practices laying the framework for many wine styles and grape varieties we still revere today.

Perhaps the greatest leap in wine's evolution pertains

to a device we still hold dear: the cork. Glassmaking technology made bottles economically feasible by the early 17th century, but credit is still due to the individual who brought bottle, cork, and corkscrew together. The invention of the cork, that little piece of tree bark, dramatically altered the wine landscape, making wine transport much easier and greatly extending a wine's life. Winemaking styles adapted accordingly, and the wine trade began to boom around Europe, and even further, as Europeans expanded abroad.

phylloxera

set

out

like a

conquistador

with

a bad

attitude,

completely

destroying

the

vines

of

europe

So it went until 1863, when the first appearance of phylloxera ravaged the wine world. Phylloxera, a root louse native to North America, reached Europe by way of steamships crossing the Atlantic. Genteel passengers on their way home from the New World brought with them the carriers: exotic plants that were all the rage. Once on shore, phylloxera set out like a *conquistador* with a bad attitude, completely destroying the vines of Europe. The wine trade was thoroughly devastated. The only cure was to replant, grafting vines onto pest-resistant North American rootstock.

modern wine

Which brings the story to the modern world of wine, a tale of science, technology, romance, and market forces. In the early 20th century, scientists such as Pasteur explained the mysteries of fermentation and pasteurization, paving the way for greater control of winemaking. The late 20th century brought unprecedented technology and investment to the vineyard; subsequently, quality levels are at all-time highs. Couple this with a thirsty global marketplace, and today's consumer has selection and variety like never before. Still, for all its colourful history, wine remains the fermented juice of grapes, a humble agricultural product to quench the thirst.

a

humble

agricultural

product

to

quench

the

thirst

wine myths

chapter two

wine

falsities abound

dispel

the

wine

myths,

friends,

and

drink

with

open

mind

and

open

mouth!

Falsities about wine abound. The abundance of wine myths is suffocating. And to what end, dear Bacchus, do we allow such untruths to be harbingers of accordance? Myths stifle our imagination; they restrain our creativity; but worse, myths hinder our wine enjoyment. Dispel the wine myths, friends, and drink with open mind and open mouth!

myth Wine gets better with age.

truth Most wine made today is meant to be drunk young. Wine collectors are getting as rare as their wines, and more and more wineries work to suit the average consumer. Your loft apartment is no place to try to age wine, so the vintage you buy now is probably the vintage you should drink now.

myth The more expensive the wine, the better it is.

truth Though we don't suggest that all cheap wine is good, a price tag is not always an accurate indicator of quality. We've had plenty of wines that have paled in comparison to others at a third of the cost. Value can be found in wines from less prominent regions and from up-and-coming wineries.

myths

nothing
to say
you can't
mix it up

myth Red wine with red meat; white wine with white meat (and fish).

truth While this may be a *general* rule, there is nothing to say you can't mix it up a bit. A fruity Pinot Noir can work well with BBQ salmon. Italians (arguably the most gastronomically inclined of all) will have white wine with beef.

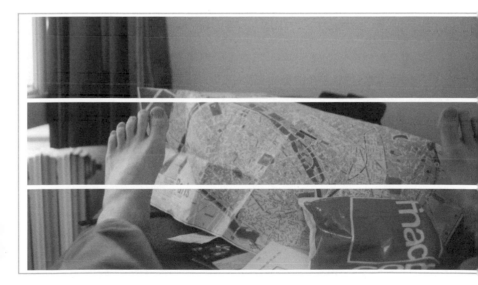

myth An 89-point wine is better than an 88-point wine.

truth Who's proposing these self-satisfying numbers? And besides, whose tongue is calibrated to a 0.01 accuracy? Wine-tasting prodigies or not, these folks are only human, and subject to their own likes and dislikes, so there's a good chance their opinions differ from yours. Trust your own tastebuds.

myth Screwtops are used on bottles of cheap wine.

truth Screwtops may single-handedly save the wine industry. Okay, this might be a bit of an exaggeration, but why this not-so-modern invention is only now being applied to fine wine is fantastically bizarre. We all love the pop of a cork, but we all hate the five percent of wine that is adversely infected by the wet cardboard smell of trichloranisole (TCA), a compound that can develop inside the natural stopper. So next time, give your loved one a bouquet of thornless roses and a screwtopped Riesling and remember that romance is subject to amenity.

myth Wine needs to breathe.

truth Wine does not need to breathe. Pop the cork (or in light of the previous myth, twist) and serve. The wine can breathe while it's in the glass if it needs to get a few sighs or gasps before you drink it.

That said, while not strictly necessary, it's never a bad idea to allow the wine to have a bit of oxygen contact before you consume it. Not all wines will improve this way, but some certainly do. But beware: opening the bottle and letting it stand upright on the kitchen counter is not letting the wine breathe. Only a very small amount of oxygen can interact with the wine this way, so you're much better off

remember

that

romance

is

subject

to

amenity

to pour it into a vessel of some sort: a proper decanter if you have one, or simply a clean water jug. And do take care how long the wine sits around in this vessel. Older wines are more delicate and can quickly lose their structure from over-exposure to the air (we're talking a half-hour or so), and while younger wines are more robust, they can suffer the same fate.

myth Use salt to clean red wine stains.

truth According to a recent UC Davis study on the removal of red wine stains (Waterhouse and Ramirez, 2001), salt is everything but effective in getting red wine out of fabric. Without making any comments about who would want to spend their free time washing cloth swatches to realize this conclusion, it does put to rest the old wives' tale. And confirms what you would have probably figured out on your own: use household stain-remover.

myth Bottles of wine should be stored horizontally.

truth Any serious wine cellar you visit will have its bottles lined up in neat little rows, lying horizontally on the shelves. This is fine configuration for the '61 Margaux and the '78 Côte de Nuits. But it's quite unnecessary for the two-year-old Napa Cab or last year's Maipo Merlot. The idea of keeping the cork moist and thus providing a good seal by horizontal storage may be appropriate for long-term ageing (i.e. five or more years), but if you're drinking these wines in the next twelve months, upright is just fine.

myth Wine needs to be served in appropriate stemware.

truth For a vast majority of the time we spent in

salt

is

everything

but

effective

in

getting

red

wine

out

of

fabric

France, we were drinking wine from small juice glasses. It tasted all right, as far as we could tell. In fact, at the end of the meal, we'd have to down the last few drops to make room for the coffee, which was poured into the same glass. And while on the topic of French table manners, it was frowned upon if we didn't relish wiping the last of the gravy from the plate with a hefty wad of bread before the table was cleared.

myth White wine should be served at fridge temperature, red wine at room temperature.

truth The temperature of your fridge is probably somewhere between 0°C and 5°C (32°F and 41°F), and too cold to appreciate most white wines. More complex whites, good Chardonnays, for example, show their best around temperatures as high as 14°C (57°F). As for reds, "room temperature" is subject to interpretation, so we like to say that 16°C (61°F) is a safe bet.

myth The bigger the punt, the better the wine.

truth First off, the punt is the dimple at the bottom of the wine bottle. It's there to catch any sediment that may have precipitated out of the wine, so when you go to pour, you get liquid and not solids. A bigger punt can probably catch bigger sediment. But just as a bigger hook can only catch bigger fish if the fish are there to be caught, these days the punt is mostly for show, as most wines you buy won't precipitate any sediment. Punt size doesn't matter; it's how you use it that counts.

punt

size

doesn't

matter;

it's

how

you

use

it

that

counts

tasting
wine

chapter three

the

toboggan

and

its

stinking

bottom

continued

to

haunt

me

throughout

childhood

I have three distinct recollections of sledding. In the first I'm a young boy, no more than five or six, with my mom and dad at one of the local mountains that backdrop Vancouver. I can't exactly remember the details, except that the wooden sleigh we used was massive, at least six feet long, and more correctly called a toboggan. The thing reeked from a tar-like substance smeared on its underside, no doubt some go-fast goo. The toboggan and its stinking bottom continued to haunt me throughout childhood, showing up in the unlikeliest of places, like our garage in Southern California.

The next memory fast-forwards to high school, during one of those long Friday nights that leave teens with idle hands. Fresh snow, a whim, and a dare; we were off to the pathetic little slopes — they can't be more than 20 metres — that bank the roadway near Vancouver Airport. We zipped down on plastic food trays borrowed from a nearby fast-food restaurant, in a fashion that would have left mothers shaking their heads.

The final memory is the most vivid, probably because it is the most recent, but I'd like to think because it involves the best wine I have ever tasted. This time I'm in the Swiss Alps, on a traditional wooden sleigh with two metal runners, classic Santa Claus style. It's mid-December and the snow is just settling in for another season.

wine

i'd been

transported

to the

front

of a

muesli

box

There's a great mountain hostel in the slopes surrounding Gimmelwald, a tiny town that's a train, bus, and tram ride away from Interlaken. Arriving there, I had the sense I'd been transported to the front of a muesli box, all picture-perfect, wholesome goodness. About as soon as I dumped my backpack, my fellow hostellers informed me that they were just on their way to the grocery store, which was a 45-minute trek up the mountain in Grindelwald. Come along, they said, and bring a sleigh.

Shortly into the hike the motivation for bringing the sleigh became apparent, with cries of "*Achtung!*" followed

and

there

amongst

new

friends

and

the

tall

peaks

of

the

alps,

I had

the

best

wine

I have

ever

tasted

by schoolkids whizzing past on sleighs. I couldn't help but notice old mattresses that had been placed as barricades on some of the more treacherous turns. After 45 minutes of perilous advance, we reached the Spar Co-op and bought sundries. Curiosity got the best of me and I found myself standing in front of the small wine section. Mostly Swiss, and mostly expensive, but on the bottom shelf was a plain one-litre (35-ounce) jug with a beer bottle crown cap. As I was pondering, a cohort sidled up, exclaimed "Ahh, Mountain Wine," and placed two bottles in her basket. She explained that not only was it merry, it happened to be the only wine a backpacker could afford in Switzerland.

We boxed our groceries and headed back out into the snow. I had been anticipating the return trip with excitement. The boxes of perishables were placed at our feet, and quick instruction and debate followed regarding sleigh-handling technique. We shoved off and I immediately utilized my new-found German language skills, *achtung* rolling off my tongue with guttural aplomb. Of course, experience soon showed itself, as some of the sledders shot out of eyesight. I contented myself with enjoying the ride, concentrating on sleigh feel and turning strategy.

Halfway down I lumbered around a sweeping right, only to be met headlong by a barrage of snowballs. Their quantity and size got the best of me, and the sleigh gave out from underneath. I looked up to see the others laughing, considered it initiation, and took the hand being offered. As I brushed off the snow, someone took out a Swiss Army knife and uncapped the crown on some Mountain Wine. The bottle was passed around, swigs were taken, and there amongst new friends and the tall peaks of the Alps, I had the best wine I have ever tasted.

tasting vs. drinking

It is important to establish early the distinction between tasting and drinking wine. The majority of wine is drunk, passing through the mouth to the gullet with little after-thought. Nothing wrong with this practice; indeed, good friends, good discussion, or even sweaty palms may prove relevant distractions from the wine. Tasting, however, permits full evaluation and added enjoyment to wine drinking.

This may at first seem counterintuitive, as convention would have us connote a *taste* as a sample, an experiment, a "taste this and tell me what you think." But in the crazy world of wine, tasting is much more. Wine really can be as simple or as complex as you want it to be, and the beauty of the grape will be enhanced through a full evaluation. In high school we never completely understood the difference between "going out" and "going steady," but we like to think that being a wine taster is like going steady with wine.

good

discussion,

or even

sweaty

palms

may

prove

relevant

distractions

super tasting women

All tasters are not born equal. It turns out that tongues—those fleshy little organs of potent repute—have varying sensitivities. It also happens that women have the majority of sensitive tongues. Personal research aside, medical studies divide the population into three categories of tasters: nontasters (25%), normal tasters (50%), and supertasters (25%). The fairer sex make up, give-or-take, two-thirds of the supertasters. Simply, supertasters are more sensitive to sweetness, bitterness, and the creamy sensation produced by fat in food.

Of course, many would say this should be obvious. Women have always been more sensitive than men, and arguably have better taste. But 21st-century, modern, sensitive man take heart, tastebud sensitivity is only one component of wine tasting. Great wine tasters are created. Some may be born with more potent tastebuds, but everyone needs a good tongue lashing on occasion.

If you must, you can unscientifically check your tasting status by counting your tastebuds. Get a clean key ring, place it on your tongue, and proceed to dab some food colouring in the mold. Now find the tastebuds in the circular area. Average tasters will count 20–40; anything more and you're a quantifiable supertaster.

infinite flavours

888

unique

flavour

sensations

So why bother tasting? They say wine's complexity is manifested in its infinite layers of flavour. While we have thus far only recorded 888 unique flavour sensations, we are nonetheless amazed at the potential for one fruit, the grape, to shed its skin and transform its taste in so many ways. The ability of grapes to ferment into such complex beverages is a significant reason why so many devote their passions, careers, and lives to wine.

Of course, numerous factors contribute to the grape's transformation, such as variety, winemaking technique, and the land in which the vines grow. The issue then is how to describe such a complex liquid. Talk of infinite flavours may seem like wine aficionado hyperbole, but the lingo underscores the need for a succinct language to help us comprehend and describe wine.

describing wine

It's a bit like going to the salon for a shampoo and trim. The question of "how do you want it cut?" is followed by gesticulations of "a little off here" and "some feathering there," the whole while you're internally pleading that the stylist shares your vision. Bringing pictures can help, but at times the whole experience begs the simple response: "make me beautiful."

The problem is that defining the qualities of a wine, like describing a hairstyle, is by nature subjective. Tasting involves our palates, which happen to be as unique as our fingerprints. Your salty may be someone else's bland, just as your latest coif could be another's mullet. Given this subjectivity, it is perfectly acceptable to describe wine using personal words. A friend once described a particular Sauvignon Blanc as being "like tiny bubbles dancing across my tongue." This proved entirely descriptive, personal, and fun to boot.

Still, the wine industry requires efficient communication, so generally accepted terminology has taken shape. Our friend's Sauvignon Blanc would be described as having "high acidity," or more attractively as being "crisp," in professional parlance. This chapter will explain the typical tasting procedure, with the ultimate goal being to leave you feeling like a wine rockstar, new haircut notwithstanding.

wine jargon:
ten terms to get you in with the wine crowd

legs
Drops of wine that appear on the inside of a glass when it's swirled. They quickly (short legs) or slowly (long legs) make their way to the wine reservoir below. Synonymous with tears.

nose
The smells of a wine. The nose is at times further broken down into aromas, smells associated with the grape itself, and bouquet, smells resulting from the winemaking or ageing process.

body
The weight of a wine in your mouth. The body of a wine can pretty much range from thin like water to viscous like syrup, denoted by the common terms light-, medium-, or full-bodied. For reference, use the handy milk analogy: light-bodied=skim milk; medium-bodied=1–2%; and full-bodied =homogenized.

length
The finish or aftertaste of a wine, including any sensations that stay with you after the wine has been swallowed (or spat). A wine that leaves a lingering taste is said to have a long finish, otherwise the wine may have a short or medium length.

well-balanced
A well-balanced wine has integrated components of alcohol, fruit, sweetness, acidity, body, and tannin (particularly if red). A balanced wine is generally seen as a well-made wine, though keep in mind balance is independent of flavour.

complex
As with people, a complex wine intrigues with innumerable layers of flavour, taste, and feel. Much preferred over a simple wine, though we strive to be simple men.

tannin
The astringent compounds found in the seeds, stems, and skins of grapes, subsequently transferred during the winemaking process.

Tannins are natural preservatives, but can be bitter if too prevalent. Tannins are also found in tea. Think of making a strong cup of black tea… now take a sip and pucker up.

dry
A wine with no detectable residual sugar. As residual sugar increases, the wine is said to be off-dry, then sweet. Be careful, however, not to confuse sweet with fruity. Many a dry wine has lots of fruitiness, but it's the residuals that determine sweetness.

big
Rather ambiguous term used to connote a full-bodied wine high in fruit, tannin, and alcohol. In other words, a wine that won't let you forget you're drinking it, even if it is not well balanced. Repeat after us: "this is a big red."

young
A wine that is not yet at its apogee, or optimum drinking stage. This docs not mean that the wine is bad, just that it might not be at its best and may develop if given time. Synonyms include tight and closed.

four-step tasting method

sticking

their

nose

deep

into the

glass

There may have been a time, say in a restaurant, when you've witnessed someone eyeing a glass of wine, swirling it vigorously, sticking their nose deep into the glass, and making unnerving slurping noises. This individual was engaged in a wine-tasting ritual and, while it may at first seem ridiculous, you'll be surprised at how quickly you can rise to the occasion.

The point of the exercise is to conduct a complete sensory evaluation of the wine, which involves sight, smell, taste, and feel. And by all means, if the wine talks to you, speaks to you in any way, then include sound as well.

Now, while some are born with superior tasting organs, overall great wine tasters are made, not born. In fact, the largest difference between experienced tasters and novices is frame of reference. You should be pleased to hear this. The more wines you taste, the larger the set of memories from which you can compare, and the easier the process becomes. As well, don't forget to smile. Why many feel obliged to appear solemn as they taste wine remains a mystery. Really, it's not as though smiles and concentration need to be mutually exclusive, especially in today's multi-tasking society.

step 1: the look

May as well start by looking at the wine. No need for a furtive glance. Go ahead, pick up the glass and give it a good once over, from stem to bowl. It helps to tilt the glass away from yourself to get a clear eyeful, perhaps holding the glass up to a white background to minimize distraction. But what are you looking for?

First, observe the colour of the wine. Wine comes in a rainbow of shades. For whites, hues range from almost water clear to deep, prairie-sun golden while reds can vary from pale through to the Pope's cardinal robe. The wine's shade helps define its style and age. As a white wine ages, it darkens in colour. The opposite is true of reds.

Also note the colour's intensity. Looking at the centre of the wine helps to gauge the depth of its brightness. Younger wines appear more vibrant, a purple tinge in reds or a green hue in whites. The intensity of colour also shows itself around the wine's edges, with brown overtones an indication of age. And no, a deep, inky red does not necessarily connote a richer wine; the original grapes

why

many

feel

obliged

to

appear

solemn

as

they

taste

wine

remains

a

mystery

could have simply been thicker skinned, or the wine may have been macerated longer to give more colour extraction.

Second, it is helpful to look at a wine's clarity. Cloudiness or evident fizz (unless it's a bubbly) would be a clear (excuse us) indication of a faulty wine. This is a rare occurrence in wine today, so don't be overly concerned. However, non-filtered wines are both tradition and trend in different parts of the world and, if not decanted properly, can show some sediment. While this winemaking debris may make for a cloudy drink, it will in no way harm the wine.

Other harmless solids that will from time to time show themselves in your glass are tartrates, more romantically referred to as "wine crystals." Tartrates are by-products of the winemaking process (handy for baking in their cream of tartar form) and have no effect on the wine's taste.

step 2: the swirl

While the swirl is the most dexterous step in the tasting process, it is entirely enjoyable. Swirling the wine coats the bowl of the glass, better arousing the wine's aromas. Small droplets called legs (also known as tears) will appear on the inside of the wineglass and run down the sides of the glass in efforts to rejoin their brethren below. Appropriately, slow-moving, thick-looking legs are said to be long, and longer legs are an indication of higher alcohol content or more residual sugar (i.e. sweeter wine).

There's no special swirling technique; a coy spin of the wrist will usually suffice. But if at first you don't succeed, start by swirling the glass on the table. We once observed the owner of a wine shop in France hold his glass mid-air with one hand, cover the top with the other hand, and proceed to shake. He explained that it better captured the

a

coy

spin

of

the

wrist

will

usually

suffice

aromas, as he wiped his hand on his jeans. You'll know you're a quantifiable wine geek when you unconsciously swirl every glass set in front of you, be it full of wine, juice, or water.

step 3: the smell

As far as body parts go, the nose gets a foul rap. From Cyrano de Bergerac to rhinoplasty, witness the obsession we have with noses: big noses, flat noses, button noses, we're all about looks! It's high time we treated the nose as the sensual organ that it is. The nose has a direct connection to the brain; indeed smells often become hard-wired to memory, and associating flavours of a wine to past memories is a handy method for description. Hence, the often-heard references to blackberry, apple, flowers, chocolate, and wood, or the even more subjective descriptors like bacon fat and petroleum jelly. The nose knows, and when tasting, we utilize our noses to a far greater degree than our tongues. Perhaps we should follow the Inuit and rethink kissing?

Smelling a wine is the most important step in the tasting process. It will do more to unlock the mystery of wine than any other evaluation, exposing its history, maturity, and character. The goal is to sense and define the aromas given by the grape as well as by the winemaking and ageing. You can count on finding a dozen or so smells in a single wine.

Trust your smelling instincts. Often your first inhale is your most honest assessment so don't be afraid to put your nose deep into the glass, nostrils wide open. And there's no shame in closing your eyes for an all-encompassing inhale. All the better to connect with your olfactory bulb.

don't

be

afraid

to

put

your

nose

deep

into

the

glass,

nostrils

wide

open

common aromas

fruit
berry, cherry, currant, boysenberry, grapefruit, lemon, gooseberry, pineapple, banana, apple, melon, peach, apricot, fig, prune

herbs and spices
black pepper, licorice, anise, clove, nutmeg, tobacco, tea, honey, eucalyptus, mint

flowers
rose petal, violet, orange blossom

earthy and woody
oak, vanilla, nutty, caramel, coffee, barnyard, dusty, mushroom, yeast

herbaceous and vegetative
green grass, bell pepper, olive, asparagus, hay

interesting
petrol, horsy, tar

unpleasant
rotten egg, burnt match, nail polish remover, wet newspaper, cabbage, mould, vinegar

not-so-common aromas

Of course, just when you think you're getting a handle on describing wine, along comes some wine writer or reviewer with some bizarre, out-of-context attempt to describe wine. Consider it proof of the subjectivity of wine tasting. Our individual palates are not only important, but valid as well. Here's a list of actual descriptors we've heard used: wet concrete, toilet bowl, pocket lint, Japanese gummies, spicy sausage, wet dog, mashed peas, pencil lead, and white glue. *And perhaps the worst of all:* funky like grandpa's drawers.

step 4: the taste

Finally, taste the wine. Tasting should let you assess flavours, and the feel of the wine in your mouth should give you a sense of its consistency. But only a proper mouthful will confirm a wine's true character. Take in a sizeable gulp, swish the wine around your tongue, slurp in air to release more smells up into your retro-nasal passage, and hope you don't choke and dribble.

finally,

taste

the

wine

The tongue's tastebuds are capable of detecting four sensations: sweet, acid, bitter, and salt, though with wine only the first three are really relevant. Sweetness from a wine's residual sugars will be detected by the tastebuds at the front of the tongue. Acidity will be picked up on the edges of the tongue. Bitterness from alcohol will be felt upon the back of the tongue. Any bitter tannins from the wine will bite the gums, causing a puckering dryness.

While the wine is in your mouth, note the tactile sensation of its consistency. The weight of a wine, commonly referred to as its body, is often determined as light, medium, or full. Swish the wine around to gauge its viscosity and detect any fizziness.

the fifth flavour element: a case for umami

A growing number of researchers maintain that our tastebuds are capable of a fifth primary taste. Along with sweet, acid, bitter, and salt, they say we also taste umami. Umami is reputed to be a savoury sensation, most commonly associated with MSG. In the years to come, umami will play an important role in wine tasting, as we learn about different levels of umami in wine. Not only will this affect wine tasting, it will influence wine and food matching, winemaking, and so on. To experience umami, try a bowl of miso soup or some vine-ripened tomatoes.

making a conclusion

Having tasted the wine and successfully swallowed or spat (under some circumstances, it does make sense to spit... we leave it up to your better judgement to determine when), you will notice the wine's flavours and personality lingering on in your mouth. This is the feel, the end of formal tasting. Now is the time to evaluate a wine's balance and finish, in general its overall quality.

A balanced wine seamlessly incorporates its components of sugar, acid, alcohol, and tannins to present a harmonious union, like a well-cast multicultural crew of a reality-based TV show. But some television programming is out of whack, and not all wines are balanced. Common traits of unbalanced wines include the not-so-subtle heat of over-pronounced alcohol, a too-tart Florida-citric zing of unbridled acidity, too much sugary goodness in a wine with unbalanced residual sugar, or a biting astringency that leaves your gums clinging to your front teeth from overblown tannins. Remember also that wines evolve over time. A wine tasting unbalanced today may be better balanced down the road, and vice versa.

Feelings can also be associated with the length of a wine's finish or its aftertaste. The finish is typically described as short, medium, or long. Finer wines inevitably have longer finishes, continuing to evoke sensory pleasures throughout the tasting process. And possibly beyond, as some would tell it. A friend once related his experience of tasting the renowned Penfolds Grange. While in Australia, he had fortunate occasion to try this powerhouse Shiraz at the winery with his wife and father. They quite enjoyed it, and proceeded home to make dinner. Legend has it that the next morning, he could still taste the wine, even after brushing his teeth. His father and wife attested to the same experience.

a

balanced

wine...

(is)

like a

well-cast

multicultural

crew

of a

reality-based

tv show

it's the wine's fault

Sadly, sooner or later in your wine-tasting life you will encounter a faulty wine. Winemaking techniques and technology have greatly reduced these occurrences, but wine is, after all, a living thing, continuing to evolve (and devolve) as it spends time in the bottle. And given our differing thresholds of perception, faults may be more or less apparent. However, when you do come across a faulty wine, chalk it up to experience and take it back. Any reputable shop or restaurant will replace the bottle.

The following are common wine faults:

corked
Common term for a wine that has been affected by cork taint, specifically a cork containing trichloranisole (TCA), a fancy name for a nasty compound that leaves wine smelling and tasting mouldy, at times like a wet newspaper.

oxidation
Too much exposure to oxygen! A wine may come into contact with excessive oxygen during the winemaking process or while sitting around in a bottle without an airtight seal. The end result is a wine that appears brownish in colour, with off-putting aromas.

vinegar
Unless a bottle has a label that reads "red wine vinegar," it is not acceptable for your wine to taste or smell sour. However, at times the presence of acetic acid created by bacterial agents will create this fault.

refermentation
The problem of yeast cells reactivating, creating an unwanted secondary fermentation in bottle. Cloudiness or unexplained fizziness hint at such a fault.

sulphur dioxide
If a wine smells like rotten eggs, it's faulty. If it has a hint of SO_2, like a just-lit match, it may blow off and the wine could be OK.

other bacteria
Countless other microscopic organisms may somehow find their way into the bottle so that, alas, when it's opened, no genie will appear.

what is a good wine?

About this time, your internal dialogue will begin to chime, "is this a good wine?" Philosophizing further with yourself may lead to variations of "when is a wine good?" or "how can I tell if a wine is good?" While in wine-taster parlance a good wine is defined as one free of faults, well balanced, with ample character and complexity, the simple answer is that a good wine is one you enjoy. Therefore, the most important task for you as a wine taster is to know what you like. And don't like. At this point you can bring the look, the smell, the taste, and the feel together to determine a wine's overall merit or detriment. Go now and taste, with confidence.

taking notes

It's worth noting the benefits gained from recording your tasting observations. Professional tasters have the habit of scrupulous note taking, but even casual tasting can be augmented by a few cursory scribbles. Yes, there are many wines out there, and try as we might, we're liable to forget. Depending on your inclination, all manner of devices are at your means: from the lowly pad of paper to a fancy wine journal complete with space for glueing removed labels.

Regardless of your chosen medium, we do recommend the strategy of at least writing down the name of the wine and a quick conclusion, such as thumbs up or down. This will keep you from adopting the annoying habit of forgetting the wines you like. Past the basics, other helpful triggers include the date of consumption, place, occasion, price... all the way to detailed notes on colour, flavour, and finish.

page from our wine tasting journal

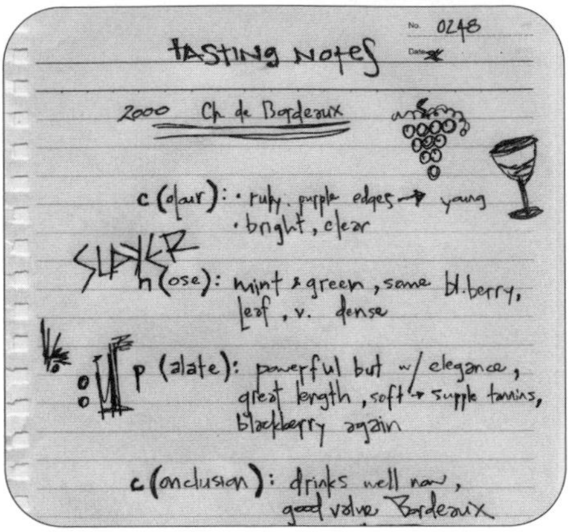

Tasting notes handwritten card:

No. 0248
TASTING NOTES   Date

2000   Ch de Bordeaux

c (olour): · ruby, purple edges → young
· bright, clear

h (ose): mint & green, some bl.berry,
leaf, v. dense

p (alate): powerful but w/ elegance,
great length, soft & supple tannins,
blackberry again

c (onclusion): drinks well now,
good value Bordeaux

experiencing wine

For all the completeness of sensory evaluation and the four-step tasting method, the best way to remember a wine is to tie it to an experience. With so much talk of tasting and drinking, it's easy to forget that the point of wine is to complement lifestyle. Remember the bottle of Chardonnay shared over a lingering dinner and blossoming romance some years ago on a warm California night? Or the seal-the-deal red Burgundy consumed during a business lunch at a Toronto restaurant? Recalling a wine brings to mind the feelings, the sentiments, the sensations of a moment. This, more than anything, completes the tasting process.

other tasting tips

Keep an open palate.
Practice makes perfect.
Don't practice alone.

guide to grapes

guide

One sunny day, summers back, I found myself lounging with a couple of good friends on a pleasant patio in Seattle. It was one of those perfect Pacific Northwest afternoons, with a sun so earnest it made me forget the more usual companionship of rain. Having spent a leisurely morning and afternoon meandering city streets, we were ready to move into evening affairs. Thankfully, summer in Seattle brings long, lazy hours of daylight, so the transition could be done at an appropriate pace.

Along with the sun-drenched patio, our locale beckoned with its extensive wine list. We stepped in to inquire about the porch and accompanying wines, and the guy behind the bar duly heeded our call. I immediately liked the place, and not only because of the unsolicited sample from an open bottle. Of course, being south of the 49th parallel, the taster was only offered after we presented proper picture ID.

Convinced this was a good place to be, we planted ourselves outside and gave a serious look through the faux leather-bound text. A half-bottle seemed sensible, and the consensus was for white. This pretty much limited us to something from France or California. As the "wine guy" in attendance, the honour of selection fell in my lap. Fair enough. I noticed a Sancerre that met our budgetary and mood requirements. I ordered the wine and sat back in my

a

sun

so

earnest

it

made

me

forget

the

more

usual

companionship

of

rain

to grapes

chair. The ensuing conversation convinced me of the need for more accessible information on wine:

me: Let's try this Sancerre.

her: [*Reasonably*] What's a Sancerre?

me: Sancerre's a region in France, of the Loire Valley.

her: [*Still not convinced*] Uh huh.

me: It's a white wine made from Sauvignon Blanc.

her: [*With a superior tone of sarcasm*] What is Sauvignon Blanc?

mc: It's a grape.

her: No kidding ... but what is Sauvignon Blanc really?

the personalities behind the wine
grapeWHAT

WHAT the grape? Different grapes have different personalities. Here, in five words or so, the typical characteristics of the most common grape varieties are defined. Use this to match a wine to your mood.

grape	WHAT?
Cabernet Sauvignon	king grape, tannic, full, ages well
Pinot Noir	cherries, silky, earthy, lighter coloured
Shiraz/Syrah	robust, peppery, powerful, lotsa fruit
Merlot	approachable, smooth, full, dark fruit
Nebbiolo	Italian stallion, bold, tar and roses
Tempranillo	juicy, berries, tobacco, dried-out to supple
Zinfandel	USA, concentrated, brambles, jammy
Sangiovese	acidic, tight, earthy, cherries
Pinotage	South Africa, unusual flavours, touch of spice
Grenache	round, smooth, floral and fruity, powerful
Cabernet Franc	nettles, herby, often found in blends
Mourvèdre	brooding, deep purple, gamy, firm structure
Carmenère	inky, fairly full, spiced plums
Malbec	dark and dirty, medium, Argentina
Chardonnay	queen grape, opulent, versatile, omnipresent
Riesling	dry to sweet, apples and limes, acidic, racy
Sauvignon Blanc	fashionable, grassy, crisp, light
Pinot Blanc	fresh, fruity, mild, drink young
Sémillon	luscious, round, big, honey
Chenin Blanc	misunderstood, at times off-dry, medium
Viognier	trendy, floral, apricot, peppy, best young
Muscat	elegant, fragrant, grapey, good dessert wines
Gewürztraminer	rich but refreshing, spicy, tropical fruits
Pinot Gris	pungent, aromatic, substantial
Pinot Grigio	same grape as Gris but Italian style and crisp
Marsanne	nutty, dry, round, honeysuckle
Torrontés	fresh, light, zesty, floral
Gamay	fruity, simple or serious, under-appreciated

Granted, describing the grapes only hints at their personalities. But remember: don't judge a grape by its skin. Growing conditions, climatic considerations, x-factors—all these contribute to create the final grape. Still, this guide offers a base to work from, a decoder ring for grape mood swings.

mainstream white grapes

chardonnay

Pity the most popular white wine grape. Chardonnay has both the fame and infamy of being #1. It makes the wine that is most widely recognized, and is probably the grape most loathed (witness the "ABC" movement—Anything But Chardonnay). Chard has a rep for being easy, as it grows almost anywhere and molds itself to a winemaker's whim and style, which also gives a clue to its potential allure. In the right hands, Chardonnay makes some of the richest, most memorable white wines in the world; however, produced without love, Chardonnay gets flabby and lifeless. *Try:*

- Unoaked, austere Chablis from France
- Buttery, voluptuous, California Chardonnay
- Ripe, melon-fruited Chardonnay from South Australia

riesling

Perhaps the purest expression of a wine grape, Riesling is a noble, if misunderstood, variety. Capable of expressive tropical fruits, floral notes, and mineral undertones, Riesling has depth and complexity. It's happy to be made dry or sweet, though its (typically) lower alcohol and lack of wood may currently make it somewhat unfashionable. Still, favours change, and Riesling can wait for its moment to shine, as finer examples have an uncanny ability—for a white grape—

to age long and gracefully. *Try:*

- Classic off-dry and supple Riesling from the Mosel, Germany
- Minerally, appley, pure Riesling from Alsace, France
- Dry, peachy, racy Riesling from Niagara, Ontario

sauvignon blanc

Known for its refreshing characteristics, Sauvignon Blanc is the grape for you if you like your wines young and fresh. It prefers growing in cooler climates, and in such environs Sauvignon Blanc maintains a bracing acidity and crisp green or citrus fruit flavour. Generally, the grape makes wines that are lighter in feel, often unoaked, though wooded examples exist and commonly go by the *nom de plume* Fumé Blanc. *Try:*

- Old-school steely Sancerre from the Loire, France
- New Zealand's famed grassy, gooseberry Sauvignon Blancs
- Heavier, melony, oaked Fumé Blanc from California

pinot gris

This pink-skinned globe has a name that translates to "grey grape." Does Pinot Gris have an identity crisis? Also known as Pinot Grigio in Italy, where the grape makes wines that are brisk and tart, the perfect aperitif sipper. Elsewhere, Pinot Gris tends towards a rounder style, often with a pungent character. It's a versatile grape that is equally at home fermenting in stainless steel or doing time in an oak *barrique*. *Try:*

- Honeyed, Tokay Pinot Gris from Alsace
- Zesty, simple, starter Pinot Grigio from Northern Italy
- Robust, lemony Oregon Pinot Gris

sauvignon

blanc

is

the

grape

for

you

if

you

like

your

wines

young

and

fresh

sémillon

A not-too-common but nonetheless important grape variety, Sémillon is a thin-skinned marvel with a mellow personality. It's the grape that inhaled! Subtle fruit aromas of fig and citrus combine with a roundness to lend Sémillon its laid-back character. Sémillon can create marvellous dry wines and (blended with Sauvignon Blanc) has a hand in some famed sweet wines as well. *Try:*

- Sweet, lush, Sauternes from Bordeaux, France
- Old, toasty and complex Sémillon from Australia's Hunter Valley
- Fun, grapey Sémillon from South Africa

gewürztraminer

Easily one of the most distinctive grapes, Gewürztraminer is like that exuberant kid with a larger-than-life personality, who at times can be amusing but then downright annoying in large doses. Hard to spell but easy to enjoy, Gewürz makes very distinctive wine, full of tropical fruits reminiscent of lychee, along with floral notes and spice. Gewürztraminer is a current darling of the wine world, with dry and sweet examples abounding. *Try:*

- Concentrated dessert Gewürz from the Rhine, Germany
- Lychee-packed, spicy Gewürz from the Okanagan, British Columbia
- Dry, rose-petal-infused Gewürz from Alsace

gewürz

is a

current

darling

of the

wine

world

mainstream red grapes

cabernet sauvignon

Arguably the most storied grape of all, Cabernet Sauvignon plays no small part in many of the world's finest red wines. The thick-skinned old man of the grape world, Cab Sauv packs a tannic punch that befits ageing. Its reputation precedes it, as vineyards the world over clamour for its small, dark berries. Cabernet Sauvignon is late ripening and therefore best suited to warmer climates, where its typical aromas of blackcurrant, green pepper, and chocolate can show through. *Try:*

- Old, mellowed Cab Sauv from California
- Tannic, powerhouse Cab Sauv from Argentina
- Eucalyptus-tinged Cab Sauv from the terra rosa soils of Coonawarra, Australia

merlot

Not just Cabernet Sauvignon's blending partner, Merlot can roll on its own skin. Ripening earlier with less tannin, the grape creates rich but soft wines, often characterized as smooth and approachable. Merlot is generally easier to get along with. The descriptions of Merlot often seem oddly sensual, ranging from supple to lush to full bodied. Teasing flavours of plum, chocolate, and berry abound. *Try:*

- Juicy, perfumy Merlot from a new-wave Southern France producer
- Luscious, plump plum Merlot from Chile
- Elegant, more obscure Merlot from Hungary

cabernet

sauvignon

plays

no

small

part

in

many

of the

world's

finest

red

wines

pinot noir

The "heartbreak grape," so called because it often causes nightmares of hardship in the winery. Pinot Noir has issues. It's demanding (preferring cooler climates for a gentle ripening), has a thin skin (which is prone to rot), and is sensitive to the soil it grows in. However, when things go right, the grape creates one of the most memorable, character-laden wines. It's then known as the "poet's wine," and many fall madly for Pinot Noir. Restrained berry fruit, mushroomy earthiness, like an iron fist in a velvet glove. Such are the wordy traits of good Pinot Noir. *Try:*

- Classic, intense red Burgundy from France
- Racy, dried cherry Pinot Noir from New Zealand
- Chewy, earthy, strawberry fruit compote Pinot Noir from Oregon

syrah / shiraz

Two names for a fabulous grape — the Aussies tend to say Shiraz, France chimes Syrah, and the rest of the world sits on the fence. Either way, it's a workhorse of a grape, easily seducing with its deep colour, numerous incarnations of fruit like blackberry, blueberry, and plum, and a peppercorn spice to kick it up a notch. Australian Shiraz tends to be potent and ripe, whereas Syrah from other parts skews to finesse and reservation. It takes well to oak, is remarkably full bodied, and will age just fine, thank you. *Try:*

- Intense, dried fruit Hermitage from France
- Ripe, fruit bomb Shiraz from the Barossa in Australia
- Potent, spicy Syrah from Washington

the

aussies

tend

to say

shiraz,

france

chimes

syrah

lesser-known white grapes

viognier

This grape's so hot it rolled down the catwalk during Fashion Week in Paris. Hope it's not just a trend because this delicate grape makes gorgeous fragrant, floral wines that work well as perfume in a pinch. Often best drunk young, with aromas reminiscent of peach-apricot *haute couture*. *Find it from:*

- California
- Australia
- Northern Rhône, France

pinot blanc

A straight-no-chaser of a grape, Pinot Blanc is as fun as a puppy dog in June. It's lower in acidity, lighter in body, with typical melon and peach aromas. *Find it from:*

- Alsace, France
- Veneto, Italy

chenin blanc

Always the star in the Loire of France, but just overcoming a bad association with plonk elsewhere, the Chenin Blanc grape is versatile and aims to please. At times lemony, at other times more honey-like, when made right Chenin Blanc has character in spades. *Find it from:*

- Loire, France
- South Africa (where it may be called Steen)
- California

muscat

Muscat is the grapey grape, which may seem redundantly redundant, but Muscat does seem most grape-like of the *vitis vinifera*. Muscat is usually made into sweet wines, from lightly tropical fizzies to strong, sticky sweet dessert wines. *Find it from:*

- Spain (known as Moscatel)
- Italy (called Moscato)
- Australia

marsanne

Fun to say twice — Marsanne, Marsanne (to the tune of U.T.F.O's old-school classic "Roxanne, Roxanne"). This grape is lower in acidity, made to be drunk now, and appreciated for its earthy, almondy, honeysuckle, big but irreverent style. *Find it from:*

- Southern France
- California
- Australia

lesser-known red grapes

cabernet franc

The other Cabernet grape, often losing its identity in Cabernet-Merlot blends though increasingly seen all by its lonesome. Cabernet Franc is a hard character to work with; if it hasn't ripened properly, it comes off leafy and brambly. When right, it's pleasingly aromatic and herby. *Find it from:*

- Loire, France
- New Zealand
- Canada

zinfandel

More or less America's patriot grape, California's Zinfandel has stirred frenzies with intense, high-alcohol brutes that pack walloping jammy, berry intensity with spice. Recently, the Zinfandel lineage has been linked to the Primitivo grape of southern Italy, and both are descendents of the Crljenak grape from Croatia. *Find it from:*

- California
- Southern Italy

malbec

Malbec's like that kid in the back of the room who lived to play D&D. It has a dark persona and seems disturbingly brooding, but once you get acquainted, you see it's quite sophisticated and pleasingly grounded, or in this case, earthy. *Find it from:*

- Argentina
- Southwest France

tempranillo

The reputation of Spanish wines pretty much rests on Tempranillo. The grape produces robust, lively reds of varying shades. Latino machismo, and aromas of leather and spice come to mind, though Tempranillo can be quite fruity as well. *Find it from:*

- Spain
- Portugal

malbec's

like

that

kid

in the

back

of the

room

who

lived

to

play

d&d

nebbiolo

The Italian stallion, Nebbiolo packs a punch like Rocky stuffs a glove. Nebbiolo reigns in Northern Italy, making huge wines of amazing depth and tarry earthiness, with typical rose-petal aromas to prove its stylish Milanese sensibilities. *Find it from:*

- Piedmont, Italy
- California

sangiovese

The Renaissance grape, Sangiovese is the versatile fruit behind the wines of Tuscany. Typical aromas offer cherry and wood spice, with a healthy kick of acidity to keep tomato sauces in check. *Find it from:*

- Italy (in general and Chianti in particular)
- Argentina

grenache

"Grenache" east of the Pyrenees in France, "Garnacha" to the west in Spain, this grape is the backbone of wines from around the Mediterranean. It is also widely used in blends and rosés for its sweet, abundant, juicy fruits that go the distance. *Find it from:*

- Spain
- France
- Australia

mourvèdre

That dark, mysterious stranger in the vineyard would be Mourvèdre. The grape seems somewhat quixotic, finicky by nature, but sufficient care and sunshine will bring compelling nuances of herbs and blackberries. *Find it from:*

- France
- Spain (known here as Monastrell)
- California

gamay

Gamay owes both its fame and infamy to Beaujolais. It's here in France where the prolific bush vines drink up the summer heat, either growing in garden variety Nouveau territory, or in the domain of one of the ten crus. Cru Beaujolais can be beautifully perfumed with ripe fruit aromas worthy of cellar ageing, whereas Nouveau (by marketing tradition it's released the third Thursday of November) makes for light, simple sipping. *Find it from:*

- France
- Canada

carmenère

Until recently, Carmenère was living in Chile under false pretences, often mistaken for Merlot. Back in its own skin, Carmenère manifests in dark, inky wines of earthy quality with ripe, plum fruit countered by spiciness. *Find it from:*

- Chile

blends

Remember the first time you realized the colour orange could be made from mixing your red and yellow finger paints? How fantastic to think that something so different, yet pleasing, would be the result. The same goes for wine: Cabernet and Merlot make Bordeaux. Combining two or more grapes to make a blended wine can—when it works—marry individual grape characteristics into a liquid of synergetic beauty. Of course, some colours don't mix well together, and ditto for grapes, so watch you don't end up with swamp mix.

marry

individual

grape

characteristics

into a

liquid

of

synergetic

beauty

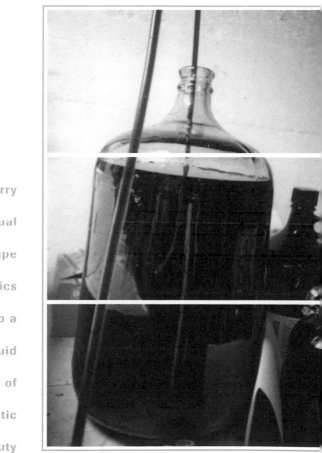

guide to pronouncing grapes

Cabernet Sauvignon	(kah-bear-NAY SO-vee-nyon)
Merlot	(murr-LOW)
Pinot Noir	(PEE-no NWAHR)
Shiraz	(shee-RAAZ) in Australia, or (shee-RAHZ)
Chardonnay	(shahr-duh-NAY)
Gewürztraminer	(gaa-VERTS-traa-MEE-ner)
Riesling	(REES-ling)
Sauvignon Blanc	(SO-vee-nyon blahn)

food
& wine
chapter five

food

The dusty train rumbled to a halt with the screech of a steel wheel on a rusty rail. It stank like beer and garbage and aftershave. Outside was dark, except for a pale blue glow that pulsated, cast by streetlights and neon signs reflecting off the grey cement. It was late summer and an oppressive humidity lay like a blanket on the skyscrapers that poked at the canopy of Tokyo.

Some time earlier I had come in from Osaka on an evening bullet train, in which, with all the seats taken by passengers who had boarded further west, I was sandwiched between women in pink suits eating kiosk sushi and men with their lips curled around limp cigarettes, letting the smoke billow from their nostrils. At Tokyo Station I had transferred to the local line, glad to finally be out of the cramped train and into the city.

I'd been living in Osaka for awhile, and though I wasn't there for reasons directly tied to wine, it seemed wine kept popping up. In Japan, of all places, I was having some peculiar wine encounters.

Some seven months earlier (I can remember the date because it involves drinking Beaujolais Nouveau—a wine released in November of every year) I was having dinner with my co-workers at a well-known seafood restaurant where massive quantities of fresh fish and shellfish came

an

oppressive

humidity

lay

like a

blanket

on the

skyscrapers

that

poked

at the

canopy

of

tokyo

& wine

the

light,

fruity

wine

was

timely

to the table to be barbecued on rustic charcoal hibachis. Beer was the going drink, but suddenly someone called the waitress over and ordered a wine. A bottle of Beaujolais Nouveau came to the table, beaming youthfulness in its near-florescence. The light, fruity wine was timely—what I call the banana bubble-gum flavour of the young wine— adding a pleasant contrast to the light smokiness of our mackerel and scallops.

The following spring on my way home from work, I stopped in at a mom-and-pop-sized liquor store not far

from the dormitory where I was living. Saké and *shochu* (potato wine, not unlike vodka) lined the shelves in the narrow, dimly lit shop, broken up by a few whiskies that looked to have been thrown in as an afterthought. A fridge hummed in a corner. Stepping further into the store, I noticed there were exactly two bottles of wine on a shelf towards the back. I picked one up and looked it over, reading the label while the proprietor explained to me it was a "Japanese wine." Made in Japan, yes, but from fruit grown elsewhere. I left with a couple cans of beer, which proved a perfect foil for my curry dinner, but to this day I regret not trying the wine, if for the experience alone.

Now I was in Tokyo to catch up with a few friends. They lived in the Ebisu district, where I was headed on the Yamanote line. Sitting across from me was a salaryman, drunk like a *daruma*. His head bobbed, his chin resting on his chest so I could see his jet-black hair, parted to match the pleat in his suit pants. On his lap rested his briefcase, a brown number with brass trim and battered corners. A couple of schoolgirls were beside me, still in their uniforms, punching madly at cellular phones sending text messages off into cyberspace. A group of guys parked near the door bragged back and forth about their successes with women.

A cry came over the intercom: Ebisu Station.

Yusuke was on a wreck of a scooter that shot blue from a hole in the side of the muffler as the machine sat idling, bouncing on dead shocks and coughing when he twisted the throttle to keep it alive. The headlamp winked. I threw my backpack over my shoulders and sat behind my friend. Yusuke had a suit on and his jacket fluttered as we tore out of the station to mix with the muggy melody of the city.

We ordered spaghetti and red wine at a place that was

his

jet-black

hair,

parted

to

match

the

pleat

in his

suit

pants

Italian, but not without its Japanese idiosyncrasies. Wrought-iron chandeliers hung over our checkered tablecloth that featured fork, knife, and chopstick. The menu offered a lot of "su-pa-geh-ti." We were on the patio, Yusuke and his girlfriend sitting on the other side of the red and white cloth, our table flanking a roadway where cars crashed along noisily and bicycles rolled by.

The spaghetti was sliding off the plate, a frictionless heap haphazardly topped with steaming meatballs and chopped garlic. We grabbed our forks and poured our wine. The carafe was still condensing from the chill of the refrigerator, making me think, "Cold red wine?" I looked at the glass and in the ruby liquid was a globular reflection of the metropolis: skyscrapers and neon signs, bending to the curvature of my wineglass. I brought the glass to my lips and swirled the wine in my mouth. And there, in the heavy, sweltering Tokyo air, I breathed in a hot mantle of city buzz that paired perfectly with cold chianti.

Kuji

what goes?

milli

without

vanilli,

wang

without

chung

It is happily inevitable that wine is consumed with food. Like Milli without Vanilli, Wang without Chung, and Kool without the Gang, food *sans* wine would be direly drab. But this is where the generalization ends. As for which wine with which food, it's not so black and white. Think of a perfect food-and-wine match and, inevitably, there will be someone to come up with an exception.

That is, there is really no hard-fast code to pairing wine with food. Though you can readily find reams of rules on the subtleties of the subject (and we'll list a few in the pages to come), the wine that you have with your meal is more to do with the wine that you feel like drinking.

And if you happen to be sitting on the southern coast of Spain watching flamenco dancers or *toreadors*, or just with your feet in the sand, a glass of sherry would probably go with anything. Just as when you're on a Qantas flight to Melbourne, how can you refuse an Aussie Shiraz? Your environment matters, too.

Finally, it never hurts to experiment. Try a challenging food and wine pairing. New styles, in food and otherwise, are always emerging, challenging the norm, and many of these are discovered on a whim.

the perfect match

However, all too obsessed with perfection, we'd be lying if we didn't say the results of your endeavours might vary. In fact, there are three different outcomes when matching food and wine.

1. *The Perfect Match:* this is when you take a bite of the food, chew it a bit, let the flavours macerate in your mouth. Then you try the wine and it's not just a liquid to wash the food back with. In the Perfect Match, the wine tangibly takes the pleasure of the food to a higher level. Tastebuds are the judge of this, and in this case they concur that the flavour of the food is elevated when ingested with the wine.

let the

flavours

macerate

in your

mouth

2. *The Partial Match:* the result of most meals. The food is served, the wine is poured, and while they don't quite complement each other perfectly, there aren't any adverse effects. The thing to remember is, though

everyone goes home happy, a tweak here and there of the flavour in the dish, or a slightly different wine choice, may have provided a Perfect Match.

3. *The Disastrous Match:* foods like asparagus, artichoke, and chili are the hardest to match. The former two wreak havoc, bringing out the worst in a wine: bitterness and greenness. The latter—the chili—numbs the tastebuds with such potency that, if the spice isn't toned down, the wine will lose nine times out of ten. Of course, there are claims that Sancerre can tame asparagus and fresh, lightly oaked Chardonnay will work with artichoke. We concede that this might be the case, but Perfect Matches they are not. For instance, whoever suggested Sauvignon Blanc with sashimi could be palatable is frankly out to lunch. We've yet to find an acceptable wine match to raw tuna save for the indigenous saké (rice wine), supporting what we say about regional food and wine.

classic pairings

There is something to be said about traditional food and wine matches. Regional food and wine seem to go so well together, there's no point in arguing differently. Almost like it was planned from the start, the fermented product of grapes grown in a certain area has an uncanny way of complementing, to surprising perfection, the ingredients that are harvested from the same place. Examples of this abound.

Lyon, France is said to be the gastronomic capital of the world. Here you can find street-side *bouchons*, the Lyonnaise café, serving pork cuts and *sabodet* and *andouillette* sausages. Of course that's breakfast. The city sits just south of Beaujolais, where the Gamay grape reigns supreme. Undoubtedly, traditional braised lamb and Beaujolais are a perfect match.

In northern Italy these days, the white truffles aren't sniffed out by pigs so much as by dogs. We suppose the dogs make for better pets. But just beyond the forested hills where truffles, black as well as white, abound, are the vineyards of Barolo. The Nebbiolo grape makes a solidly bold wine, with a distinct earthiness. An earthiness not unlike truffles. The two delicacies pair well.

To put to rest the idea that only heavy red wine goes with heavy meats, there is no better match for *kasseler rippchen*, German smoked pork, than German Riesling. The honey and apple flavours of the delicate off-dry wine parlay the slightly dry, dense meat. Dump some sauerkraut on the pork and it will play off the acidity in the Riesling. Slop some potato salad or red cabbage on the side and you've got a meal.

It seems that every restaurant in Spain has a different version of *paella*. Whether it's more or less olive oil, more or less saffron, or made by a man or a woman (an old saying explains only men can make good paella), it's hard to say. But sitting on the east coast of Spain, the home of both paella and cava, dissecting a garlic-marinated shrimp with a glass of the sparkling wine might be as close to *una paella como dios manda* (a paella as God intended) as you can get.

modern pairings ────────────────────

On the other hand, there is no denying that we're hurtling towards new frontiers in cuisine. And isn't globalization a

undoubtedly,

traditional

braised

lamb

and

beaujolais

are a

perfect

match

wonderful thing when we can get Clarks, the staple of English footwear, made in Portugal, good, down-home computers like IBM made in Taiwan, and the best-selling Japanese beer, Asahi, made in the Czech Republic? And while we shuffle our feet in our suede shoes and tap-tap on our notebooks, we can look forward to salmon cakes and spring rolls for dinner. "Modern" and "fusion" are two of our favourite buzzwords.

"modern"

and

"fusion"

are

two

of

our

favourite

buzzwords

These fantastic flavours of fusion interject a fresh dimension of personality into our food. However, since the national origins of these comestibles are often not traditional sources of wine, for the wine drinker (who won't settle for beer with a meal) it adds a challenge to come up with food and wine matches that work. Some very interesting pairings have come out of theory, experimentation, and a bit of luck, granting us globalized meals of venerable breadth.

Indian curry has an infallible spice that needs some taming, quite out of the reach of a typical Chardonnay or Cabernet. Look to Gewürztraminer's lychee and floral off-dry flavour to cut through the curry by way of agreeable contradiction.

Thai cooking also incorporates some pretty serious seasoning, and while on par with the intensity of Indian curry, it is void of the richness of heavy meats and sauces. Not to say that Gewürztraminer would be a bad choice (don't knock it till you've tried it), but a wine with less weight and a bit more punch would work. A New World Sauvignon Blanc might do the trick, particularly a fresh, recent vintage that comes as a lighter-bodied white, but is uncompromising in its citric devotion.

Not so spicy is dim sum, coming to the table concealed in woven baskets pushed on metal carts. Wrapped as a dumpling, the dominant flavours are pork and seafood, with an unmistakably oily component. We only wish more Chinese restaurants had bold Italian Barbaresco on their wine list. The brilliance behind this pairing is that, despite being a full-bodied red, Barbaresco has an endearing soft, velvet quality over a fast acidity that cuts through the thickness of the dumpling and meshes with the savoury elements of the meat.

look to

gewürztraminer's

lychee

and

floral

off-dry

flavour

to cut

through

the

curry

by

way of

agreeable

contradiction

66

grapeWHEN

Matching wines to food is akin to accessorizing an outfit. You want every-thing to go together, but that doesn't mean you have to be obvious. And there're bonus points for creativity. Some suggestions:

grape	WHEN?
Cabernet Sauvignon	steak, dark chocolate
Pinot Noir	grilled salmon, roast chicken, mushrooms
Syrah/Shiraz	lamb with rosemary, kangaroo filet
Merlot	baba ganoush, Camembert
Zinfandel	nachos, chili, teriyaki
Pinotage	caramelized onions, felafel
Cabernet Franc	goulash, pulled pork sandwiches
Mourvèdre	BBQ ribs, lamb chops with herbes de Provence
Carmenère	alone, late at night
Malbec	slow-grilled food, cabbage rolls
Gamay	picnic, tacos
Sangiovese	pizza, lentils, tomato sauce
Tempranillo	ravioli, pork loin, chorizo
Nebbiolo	osso buco, stew
Chardonnay	Caesar salad, crabcakes, guacamole
Riesling	turkey, applesauce, hot and sour
Sauvignon Blanc	jumbalaya, shellfish, tuna sandwiches
Sémillon	prawns, blue cheese
Chenin Blanc	basil, zucchini fritters, baked yam
Viognier	grilled whitefish, houmous
Gewürztraminer	curry, ginger, hotpot
Pinot Gris	potato salad, borscht, smoked salmon
Pinot Blanc	goat cheese, mussels
Port	with a book
Champagne	in the bath with mango and a friend

the rules

So there are some rules to pairing wine with food. In fact, a regular constitution of wine rules has been written and re-written by a host of wine-ies and foodies, trying to put their plump digits on material facts to bombard their readership with. Some of the concepts are legit, some are *complètement fou*. In short, there are two principles in pairing wine to food:

1. *Match* the taste, texture, flavour, and intensity.
2. *Contrast* the taste, texture, flavour, and intensity.

the trouble with spice

Whether we're talking cayenne or kimchee, spice is nefariously difficult to pair with wine. Why? The *capsaicin* (the hot compound in the chili) anesthetizes your tongue so you can no longer detect flavours, particularly the delicate flavours of wine. Rendered nearly bland, the wine comes across as harsh (from the alcohol) and tannic (if it's a red wine), both undesirable qualities that would have been masked had you had your taste faculties. How do you beat the heat? Curb the spice and pick a low-alcohol, low-tannin wine.

taste

Recall that the human tongue is able to identify four different tastes: sour, sweet, salty, and bitter. These are sensed by four different parts of the tongue, but when you have something in your mouth, they all work in unison to convey the overall taste.

When applied to food and wine, however, it works to consider the four separately, under the philosophy of either matching or contrasting.

Sour.

In most cases, matching a high acid wine with an equally acidic food is a good strategy. As a successful pair, one won't dominate over the other. For instance, vinegar is a notorious problem for its overbearing acidity, but keep it to small doses and the acidity will play well with a wine of equal rancour. And if the sharp, caustic Sauvignon Blanc is kicking the shit out of your halibut, drip a bit of lemon juice on the fish to bring the acidity into check.

Sweet.

If your dessert is sweeter than your dessert wine, it could spell trouble. You'll take a bite of the dessert, then a sip of the wine, and the latter will be a flat mouthful of alcohol. The food will have climatized your tastebuds to a sweetness level, and the lesser sweetness in the wine will have all but disappeared in the shadow of the dessert. A better option is to have a dessert wine that is a notch sweeter than the food and, conversely, the wine will be less cloying after the dessert. Here there will be a pleasant finish to the food–wine combo. Again, if you're in a bind, and the dessert is obviously sweeter than the wine, try a few drops of lemon on the dish to allow the wine's sweetness to show through.

Salty.

The contrast between saltiness and sweetness has its roots back in traditional cuisine. Is there a better pairing than fois gras and Sauternes (sweet wine from Bordeaux, made from grapes affected by sugar-concentrating botrytis)? Or blue cheese and port? To match salt and salt, though, try salted nuts with a fino sherry. Though sherry isn't salty, as wines generally aren't, its unique flavour gives a perception of such.

matching

a

high

acid

wine

with

an

equally

acidic

food

is a

good

strategy

Bitter.

Bitter might be the least popular of the four tastes. Bitter food is usually helped along by sweetness or saltiness, added in the form of a sauce or similar cloaking device. The rarity of bitter food is only matched by that of bitter wine, as in an ideal world, any bitterness in the drink (coming from tannins or alcohol) is masked by the wine's more amiable qualities.

tricks of the trade

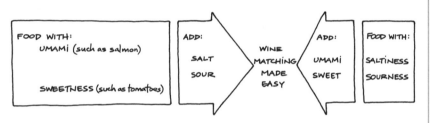

FOOD WITH:
UMAMi (such as salmon)

SWEETNESS (such as tomatoes)

ADD:
SALT
SOUR

WINE
MATCHING
MADE
EASY

ADD:
UMAMi
SWEET

FOOD WITH:
SALTINESS
SOURNESS

examples

The classic example is fresh, West Coast sockeye. Whether it's oven-baked or BBQ-grilled, touch it up with a sprinkle of salt and a squeeze of lemon. Both of these additions move the fish into the zone where its new-found balance can pair with a wide range of wines, even an unexpected, fuller-bodied red.

Vine-ripened tomatoes have a distinct sweetness and, to top it off, are good proponents of umami. Chop and mix them with slices of buffalo mozzarella, fresh basil, and olive oil. Add a dash of salt and they're ready for nearly any wine you throw at them.

texture

The texture of food is an elusive property. In fact, we don't think about the texture of our meal very often. Nonetheless, texture is a key point when matching food and wine. It is affected not only by the ingredients used, but also by the way the dish has been prepared. Poached will feel different from fried. Fried will feel different from grilled.

For the most part, the textures of food and wine should match: a light dish with a light wine, and a rich dish with a heavy wine. A poached white fish with a Gavi (a steely white from northern Italy), and a creamy pasta with an oaky Chard (California is good for these).

get a feel for it

cooking method	wine choice
Steamed: delicate, flavour intact	Lighter, fruity white: Pinot Blanc
Stewed: hardy, flavours meshed	Sturdy red or big white: Chardonnay
Grilled: charcoal, smoky flavour	Full, fruity red (fruit will contrast the smoke): Malbec
Roasted: tender, strong flavours	Robust, but not overly fruity, red: Nebbiolo

flavour

The flavour of a dish is a little more obvious. It can come in the form of the main ingredients—the meat, the vegetable, or otherwise. Say you're having quail or pheasant, main ingredients that are particularly gamy. Try matching this prominent flavour with an earthy, gamy Rioja. Or, if there's toffee tiramisu for dessert, serve a sweet Muscat that personifies a matching caramel flavour. A grilled steak, heavy in charcoal flavours, is contrasted well by a bold, fruity Cabernet Sauvignon. Rather than getting bogged down in coarse flavours, the fruit in the Cab can lift the weight of the steak.

the trouble with tannins

Tannins, the compounds behind the bitter hit that binds your lips to your teeth, are not the most food-friendly characters. Salty foods amplify tannins. Tannic wines make fish taste metallic. They make sweet food bland and don't play well with acidic dishes.

But it's not all doom and gloom. If you need to tame your tannins, try a juicy steak whose poignant protein will settle any puckering disagreement.

Bridge Ingredients.

Then the waiter comes along and grinds black pepper all over your plate. Suddenly you not only have grilled meat, now you've got grilled, spicy meat. The Cab may have to be sidelined for something else. Maybe a full-bodied, jammy Shiraz with its characteristic spicy kick would work, playing off the ground pepper. Here, a second ingredient, the pepper, has come into the picture and created a bridge to the peppery wine.

Using a secondary ingredient—like a simple spice—is a legit way to force a match, or a bridge, between food and wine. If you're serving lamb for instance, include a mint sauce, and pour a Merlot that has a hint of eucalyptus flavour. They could complement each other well. Mashed potatoes are an infallible standby side dish. But try sprinkling some toasted pine nuts into the recipe and serve with a barrel-fermented Chardonnay. The oak flavour in the white wine will respond to the nuttiness and you'll have a better chance of playing matchmaker.

cooking with wine

Tying food to wine using this flawless formula is always a good way to go. Many recipes call for a bit of wine and, even if they don't, it probably wouldn't hurt to add a bit. And by serving the same wine at the table, you've automatically moved towards a match. The classic example is beef bourguignon, where the meat is cooked in a red wine sauce. Burgundy (Pinot Noir) works well. Then this Burgundian styling gets highlighted when you take a sip of the same wine.

However, too often people think cooking with wine requires cooking wine. Not so. If you're looking for wine to add to your cooking, don't go rummaging through the cupboards for that old, nasty wine that was opened last year and never finished. The flavour of the wine will show up in the food, so make sure you use one that you'd just as soon drink from a glass.

intensity

Finally, it is important to notice the intensity of the food. Revisiting the steak, it's a beast, brazen on the plate in front of you. There's no denying its dauntless presence. To go with this, the Cab (or Shiraz) provides an intense, full flavour, strong enough to stand up to the bold meat. Matching intensity is another thing to keep track of.

A dish light in texture and delicate in flavour, like briny Pacific oysters, screams for a wine with finesse and subdued flavour. Chablis (Chardonnay from northern Burgundy) will work. Japanese dishes (other than sashimi), though equally light in texture, have the more intense flavouring of miso or soy sauce. While they would need a wine with a similarly light body, a bigger flavour would be required to balance everything out. Try a Riesling.

mimi's recipes

Not many people we know embody the spirit of the Good Life like Mimi. A serious cook, engaging conversationalist, and lover of wine, she's the teacher and we are the pupils. Literally, since Mimi is a retired high school home economics teacher (you have to respect anyone who has the prowess and patience to teach teenagers how to cook). Her commitment to good taste is unfaltering, and she happens to be the only person we know who cares enough to grow her own garlic, season her own seaweed, and harvest her own wool. So, we knew just who to turn to when we needed some recipes.

Pa Amb Tomaquet (Toasted Bread with Tomato)
From the streets of Barcelona comes this comfort food, dead easy to make and simply satisfying. Using Mimi's homegrown garlic and tomatoes, it doesn't get much better.

    12 slices cut from a loaf of rustic bread
    6 tomatoes, the riper the better
    3 cloves garlic
    olive oil
    salt and pepper

method
Toast the bread. Halve tomatoes and garlic cloves crosswise. While toast is warm, rub 1/2 garlic clove all over one side. Squish on 1/2 a tomato, letting seeds and pulp soak into bread. Dribble on olive oil. Toss on salt and pepper.
Note: If desired, thin-sliced ham works wonders.

wine accompaniment
The strong garlic influence and acid in the tomatoes scream for a wine with pizzazz. If you want to keep this a regional pairing, opt for sparkling cava (bubbly is so versatile). If you feel like red, consider Italian chianti, which is typically high in acidity and therefore a good match with the tomatoes.

Homemade Sushi Cones

Sushi literally means vinegared rice, and making it is a damn fine way to spend a night with decent company. Get your friends together, gather round the table with a big pot of sushi rice, some *nori*, lots of different fillings, and roll away. It takes a bit of practice, but makes for good conversation.

4 cups (1 L) short grain rice
5 cups (1.25 L) water

sushi *su* (marinade)
⅓ cup (80 mL) rice wine vinegar
5 tbsp. (75 mL) sugar
2 tsp. (10 mL) salt
1 package nori (seaweed)

for serving
wasabi
soy sauce
Japanese mayonnaise
pickled ginger

fillings
ebi (prawns)
unagi (eel)
crab sticks
smoked salmon
cucumber
steamed asparagus
baby corn
toasted sesame seeds

method
Wash and rinse rice a few times to remove starch. Drain, add water, and cook. Combine marinade ingredients. Empty hot rice into sushi *oke* (bamboo container) or a large bowl. Mix in the marinade, fanning the rice to cool and give it a shine. Cut nori into 4 x 7½ inch (10 x 19 cm) rectangles. Spread marinated rice along one side of nori. Fill with desired ingredients. Roll into cones. The point should be the middle of the longer side (it takes practice). Serve with the wasabi, soy sauce, Japanese mayonnaise, and pickled ginger.

wine accompaniment
Sushi is tricky to pair with wine, since there's a party of flavours going on: sweet and sour rice, rich fillings, salty seaweed. Still, we're always up for a good challenge, and we make sushi while drinking Sauvignon Blanc, for its snappy, crisp qualities. As well, we've found slightly off-dry Riesling to work marvellously; it not only has high acidity like Sauv Blanc but also residual sugar, mimicking the vinegar and sugar marinade.

Curried Chicken, Mimi Style

There are three great things about this dish. First, it's tasty in a "warm the body" kind of way. Second, the aromas that it spews while cooking are divine. Third, leftovers taste even better the next day.

2–3 tbsp. (30–45 mL) curry powder, or to taste
1/2 tsp. (2 mL) turmeric
1/2 tsp. (2 mL) powdered ginger
1/2 tsp. (2 mL) paprika
3–4 tbsp. (45–60 mL) butter or vegetable oil
2 cloves garlic, minced
1 large onion, chopped
1/2 cup (125 mL) celery, chopped
1/2 small jalapeño pepper, minced
2 lbs. (900 g) boneless chicken thighs, cut into 1 inch (3 cm) pieces
2 tbsp. (30 mL) flour
1/2 cup (125 mL) dry white wine
salt and pepper to taste

method
Heat heavy pan until hot. In the pan, toast the curry, turmeric, ginger, and paprika a few minutes until fragrant and set aside. Heat butter or oil in same pan. Add garlic, onion, celery, and jalapeño, cooking until soft. Add 1/2 the spice mixture and coat vegetables. Set aside. Add chicken to same pot and brown. Coat chicken with remaining spices and cook through. Add vegetables and flour, stirring thoroughly. Pour in wine and simmer covered until meat is tender, about 1 hour. Season with salt and pepper.
Note: Serve over rice or with chapati, along with any condiments: chutney, toasted coconut, mandarin orange sections, chopped green onion, chili flakes, yoghurt.

wine accompaniment
We won't be offended if our guests reach for beer, but curry goes with wine as well. Usually it's the spice in curry that kills the wine, so in this recipe the heat has been toned down to make it wine friendly. Stick to fruity, low-tannin wines. We'd drink Gewürztraminer or a rosé.

Pepper Steak Au Vin

Not enough people seem to de-glaze these days, and we can't understand why. Throw in some wine, scrape all the goodness off the bottom of the pan, and be done with it. Much easier than a gravy.

4 steaks, tenderloin if you're flush, but any boneless cut works
lots of fresh, coarse ground pepper
1-2 tbsp. (15-30 mL) vegetable oil
red wine

method
Remove steaks from fridge, let come to room temperature, about 1 hour. Grind a mound of pepper, using a mill or mortar and pestle. Generously coat pepper on both sides of each steak. Heat heavy frying pan to hot but not smoking. Add oil. Cook steaks to desired doneness. Remove steaks and add a glass of red wine to pan. De-glaze, stirring until sauce thickens. Plate and pour sauce over steaks.
Note: For a vegetarian version, use portobello mushroom caps. Just remember to brush caps with olive oil so the pepper will stick.

wine accompaniment
Time for big red. Cabernet Sauvignon or a Meritage blend would be classic choices. If we were feeling really saucy we'd uncork a bottle of peppery Shiraz, which would match the pepper rub.

Warm Pasta Salad

An easy dish that takes no time at all, perfect for most nights of the week. Done in 20 minutes flat, as long as you chop the veggies while the pasta water is boiling.

2 cups (500 mL) dried pasta, penne or rotini works well
1/3 lb. (150 g) Brie, cut into 1/4 inch (0.5 cm) pieces
2 cloves garlic, minced
1/2 small onion, minced
1/4 cup (50 mL) olive oil
2-3 Roma tomatoes, cut into 1/2 inch (1 cm) cubes
1 package/ bunch fresh basil, chopped
2-4 tbsp. (30-60 mL) fresh parsley, chopped
salt and pepper

method
Cook pasta. Drain, and while still hot add Brie, garlic, onion, and olive oil. Toss to melt cheese. Add tomatoes, basil, and parsley. Season with salt and pepper.
Note: If fresh tomatoes are not available, use canned. Likewise, dried spices work in a pinch. Finally, for a sweeter, mellower flavour, sauté onion and roast garlic beforehand.

wine accompaniment
The Brie is the main consideration here. A full, robust Chardonnay would match the creaminess of the cheese. Reds generally have a harder time with soft, rich cheeses, but if in the mood, we'd fancy a fruity Grenache, preferably old-vine for some down-home character.

wine and cheese

Wine and cheese: throw in some crusty bread and you've got a meal. Skip the starch and you still have a snack. Wine and cheese is a pairing with a decadent legacy. Sadly, if there's one thing many fear more than wine, it's cheese. While it's true that cheese has nuances, smells, and intricacies, it's equally true that it doesn't take much to get past the rind. Thankfully, a geographic coincidence brought us to *Les Amis du Fromage* in Vancouver. *HALFAGLASS* was birthed up the street from this corner *fromagerie*, and on the occasion of grilled cheese for lunch we headed down the block. Inside we were met by a cacophony of smells and ripening wheels. We also met Alice Spurrell and her merry crew of cheese merchants. It was eye-opening. We left with not only some aged cheddar (white, not orange!), but also a new-found respect for the world of cheese.

We've been going back regularly since, and the staff never fail to impart some wisdom on the wonders of *fromage*, be it cow, goat, or sheep.

So it was a no-brainer to head over and see Alice when it came time for some advice. We sat on stools in the back as Alice cut the cheese, surrounded by hunks and wedges of soft and hard, furry and holey, smelly and tasty delights. We asked her to suggest five types of cheese that would work well as a primer, and five more for those ready for the heady stuff. As a bonus, she recommended cheeses to try with bubbly.

the daily rinds

Brie de Meaux
A great starter cheese, Brie is versatile and omnipresent!
It's made from cow's milk, is creamy, French in origin, and
as it matures it takes on nutty characteristics.
Match with: just about any wine

Cave-Aged Gruyère
From Switzerland, Gruyère is a hard cheese from cow's
milk. The cave-ageing gives it a little zip of nut and smoke.
Match with: most reds and whites

Beaufort
A semi-hard, rich cheese from France, it's a product of the
famed mahogany-coloured bovines of the same name.
Match with: goes really great with port

Manchego
From the wide-open La Mancha plateau of Spain, this is a
hard cheese with a full, soft flavour. Made from sheep's milk.
Match with: whites, reds, anything

Explorateur
A cheese with a great spaceship label, Explorateur is named
in honour of the first U.S. satellite. Past the wrapping it's a
soft, very rich cheese of cow's milk.
Match with: fruity reds, Riesling and other fruity whites

challenging curds

St. Felicien
Creamy and soft, this cheese is from the Rhône-Alpes of
France, made from cow's milk.
Match with: white Rhône wines

explorateur

is

named

in

honour

of the

first

u.s.

satellite

Appenzeller-Extra

From the northeastern part of Switzerland, the Extra suffix means this is an Appenzeller with oomph, semi-hard and made from cow's milk.

Match with: red wine in general

Ossau-Iraty

In the western French Pyrenees lie the towns of Ossau and Iraty. Their namesake semi-hard cheese is produced from the herds of sheep that graze from the valley to the hillsides.

Match with: Gewürztraminer, or other whites

Provolone Picante

Provolone is well known, a semi-hard Italian cheese of cow descent, found in many a panini or four-cheese pizza. But we're talking Provolone Picante, the next level, an incarnation with incredible zing.

Match with: big reds like Barolo or Bordeaux

Sainte Maure de Touraine

A curious-looking hard cheese from France, Sainte Maure is made from goat's milk, set into a log shape, and subsequently rolled in black wood ash for ageing.

Match with: most whites, but stay away from Riesling and Gewürztraminer

bubbly bonus

Yes, you can have your cheese and sparkling wine too. So, as you find yourself popping the cork on a bottle of bubbly, try reaching for these.

Parmigiano Reggiano

Yep, the same stuff you grate over your pasta, but easier to eat in chunks with a flute of bubbly.

yes,

you

can

have

your

cheese

and

sparkling

wine

too

L' Edel de Cleron
A soft, cow's milk cheese from the Franche-Comté region of France.

Chaource
Another rich beaut produced from the milk of French *vaches*.

other tips

- Keep in mind that quality cheese comes at a premium price. Buy smaller quantities, you'll still end up ahead.

- Much like food and wine, great wine and cheese matches are elusive. Wine and cheese change over time, a perfect match happening only when both are consumed at the right stage.

- Write down the names of cheeses you try. Many can be confounding, or at least foreign.

buying &
collecting
wine

They were carefree times that, strangely enough, coincided with drinking healthy amounts of wine. Mostly red, and not for health benefits (the reports had yet to be widely published), but rather because it was all I knew. That, and red wine was a good base for sangria.

Under the pretext of a student exchange programme, I found myself living in a working-class neighbourhood of L'Eixample, Barcelona. I was two blocks from Gaudí's *La Sagrada Familia*, in a city that oozed life from every edifice, where an organic sense of living echoed in the curvaceous spires of the famed architect's cathedral. From my fourth-floor apartment I would watch the city unfold, glass of wine in hand. It was here that I became acquainted with strong coffee, gained some proficiency in Spanish, partied late, and learned to love wine.

It was simple, really. I saw how food and wine were incorporated into culture, the paired result creating an apparent zest for life. My young and stoic North American eyes got all misty in delight. Standing in front of a wall of wine at our little local supermarket, my roommates and I decided to indoctrinate ourselves. With grand ideas and student budgets, we set out to find the best bottle of cheap wine. We started at the bottom, and worked upwards, peseta by peseta. It was a commitment to lifestyle. Wine

barcelona ...

a city

that

oozed

life

from

every

edifice

wine

was to be an everyday occurrence in our ex-pat household.

there

were

large oak

barrels

hugging

the ceiling

We eventually found our wine, but only by accident. It was waiting in the rafters of a tiny general store around the corner, and if it weren't for a local walking in while we were browsing the bottles on the shelves, we would never have known. The Barcelonian exchanged pleasantries with the shopkeeper, pointed upwards, and subsequently left with a big jug of red wine. We looked up and sure enough, there were large oak barrels hugging the ceiling.

The ordering process proved uncomplicated, as there

were only four wines to choose from. Once we had decided upon "strong dry red," "lighter red," "dry white," or "off-dry white," it went something like this:

"¿Qué tipo?"

"Vino tinto y seco."

The dry red wine was ours. The *dueño*, or owner, headed to the back and returned bearing a plastic bottle, one that previously had seen duty as a soft drink or bottled-water container. The appropriate hose was tapped and the wine flowed free. The minimum purchase was 1.5 litres (52 oz), and the cost was always 300 pesetas. Then it was back round the corner to our apartment, furnished way ahead (and behind) its time in textbook 1970s décor: off-white shag rug, modular furniture covered in green velour, geometric calendars galore. It was enough to make us spend most of our time on the small balcony. There we retired, Coke bottle full of wine in one arm, grammar book in the other, to sit on our perch and practice our past tense, irregular verb conjugations.

the rules

Unfortunately, for many, the act of buying a bottle of wine is only slightly more enjoyable than a trip to the dentist and a nudge less nerve-wracking than the purchase of a box of prophylactics. Of course, it shouldn't be this way. In our ideal world, the wine-buying experience would reference shopping at the Italian *enoteca* of yore; a one-stop gourmet shop selling fresh, prime, quality sundries, with a little gossip on the side. Not only could you stop by for some wine, you could pick up the fixings to compliment. Instead, intimidation, lack of knowledgeable staff, and overzealous marketing campaigns seem to belittle the entire wine-buying process.

As we step down from our soapbox, we'll offer the notion that confidence goes a long way in the wineshop. The best way to gain this confidence is to have practical information. Whether you buy wine at a supermarket, government liquor store, or specialized wine retailer, some general knowledge will make the process more enjoyable.

the *HALFAGLASS* wine-buying method

It's important to develop an inner dialogue. Whenever we enter a wineshop, we systematically mumble to ourselves three little questions before selecting a bottle:

What mood am I in?

How will this wine be drunk?

How much is in my pocket?

a balanced budget

Just as with any purchase, it helps to have an idea of what you want before you shop. Are you buying a Monday night bottle? Or a gift? Or something to take to dinner? There is a wine for every budget and for every occasion, and a bit of premeditated thought will keep you from second-guessing. There's no reason to feel cheap about walking out with a $10 bottle of wine. There's also nothing wrong with asking for help. If you find a shop with knowledgeable staff, they'll delight in dispensing their opinion. They may even turn you on to a new type of wine.

price vs. quality

It's no secret that in North America wine is seen as a luxury good. As a consequence, we tend to equate a higher price with a better bottle of wine. While it's true that great wines can set people back a week's worth of groceries, the $10 bottle may also esteem to greatness. Drinking only $100 wine is fine and encouraged if it makes you feel intrinsically better, but don't sit next to us and begin to spew on some high-priced wine ego trip.

It's better to use value as the reference point. Granted, value is a more ambiguous metric, but we've found there are two valuable things worth hunting for: love and wine. Though you can't put a pricetag on love, a good wine-buying strategy is to seek out undervalued wines. Wine, in its fashionable way, is subject to trends, and popularity puts upward pressure on prices—dramatically, if the supply is limited. Stay ahead of (or don't follow) the trends and you'll find some bottles with prices aching to please.

To give some context, during the 1980s to early 1990s, bad clothes and Merlot were hot (we solemnly swear to never again peg our pants). Depeche Mode drank Chardonnay and prices for these wines kept pace with the miniskirts, rising higher and higher. For the 2000s, Shiraz is the new Merlot, and, well, Chardonnay is the new Chardonnay. Clothing styles will always be questionable, but thankfully baggy pants and Flock of Seagulls have dropped under the radar.

What's around the corner? Wines made from Malbec and Gewürztraminer are gaining a following. What is undervalued? Chenin Blanc needs a new PR agent, but until it finds one, bargains can be found. Eastern Europe,

there

are

two

valuable

things

worth

hunting

for:

love

and

wine

in particular Hungary, is showing some good whites. Reds from southern France and Italy are bold and beautiful but not so brazen on the pocketbook.

laid out _____

When we walk into a store, we first try to establish how the wine is organized. It's not like there is necessarily one correct approach, but it's important that some sort of theory, besides chaos, is at work. Wines in a shop may be organized by grape type, or perhaps by region. A few progressive retailers categorize by style, say "light and fruity white" or "smooth and soulful red." Whatever, as long as once the layout has been assessed, any particular bottle of wine is easy to find.

message on a bottle _____

The underground music scene revels in the trade of "white labels": DJ-only copies of soon-to-be-released music that contain no artist info on either the record or the sleeve. Wine bottles, on the other hand, though they may spin just as nicely, should not have blank labels. Domestic labels are pretty straightforward and easy to understand. However, as with great music, a lot of great wine is imported and you may draw blanks when peering at wine labels on the shelves, lost in a foreign *lingua* mishmash akin to wine Esperanto. And let's be honest here, we're mostly referring to Old World wines, in particular those from Germany, France, and Italy.

Learning a little will broaden your wine experience—a lot. The Old World chapter will provide fluency in foreign wine labels, but as a primer, consider the following: wines

lost

in a

foreign

lingua

mishmash

akin

to

wine

esperanto

from these countries have traditionally been named after regions, as opposed to grape types. So you find place names on the labels, such as Bordeaux or Hermitage, as opposed to the grape names, which would be Cabernet-Merlot or Syrah, for instance. Too many people miss out on Old World wines because they don't understand the labels.

wine scores and accolades

We've never met a 100-point wine we didn't like. Then again, on a 100-point scale, a top score would connote perfection, and we've never met a perfect wine. Certain wines have moved us like our first watch of *Transformers: The Movie*, but even that gem had some rough cuts.

Nowadays, it's nigh impossible to buy a bottle of wine without being subjected to wine scores. The 100-point wine scoring system was popularized by Robert Parker Jr., a no-holds-barred wine taster from America who publishes the *Wine Advocate*. Call it North American fascination with numbers, call it effective information chunking, but the 100-point system has proven a succinct, objective way to discuss wine, and consumers have leapt on the scoring bandwagon. Now everyone, from major wine publications to the corner grocer, awards points to wine.

Complementing the numbers are wine awards. There you are, standing in front of a wall of wine, confused as hell, when you notice a sticker professing "Gold Medal Winner." Everybody wants a winner, so why not go for the gold? But before you simply grab the bottle with the award, take a moment to consider the scope of the contest, the judges, how many different wines were entered, etc. The number of wine awards continues to escalate like corporate bankruptcy rates and their reliability may be as lax as

everybody

wants

a

winner,

so why

not go

for

the

gold?

corporate accounting practices.

The problem, of course, is that wine is subjective, taste is individual, and palates are personal. Attempting to fit wine into an objective framework begrudges the entire experience, hinders experimentation, and generally stifles, like many of mainstream Hollywood's attempts at creativity.

While we don't deny that these systems communicate information about wine to consumers, we worry about their overall effect. We encourage you to take a risk. Be your own critic. Buy the bottle that scored 86 points, even if there's another of the same price that scored an 88. Better yet, buy a wine that's yet to be rated; chances are when it does receive a favourable review, the price will climb. Buy a bottle because it has a pretty picture on it. Pick up the bottle that speaks to you. The point is to trust your judgement. Use scores and awards as a guide, but not as divine scripture.

things that make a wineshop great

Plainly, it sucks that buying wine can be a difficult process. Depending on your jurisdiction, bureaucracy may conspire to limit your buying options. Government-run liquor stores may be your only source. Otherwise, high-volume retailers such as supermarkets or online wine sites will generally offer the most discounted prices. Buying direct from the winery is a good way to get in on the latest offerings. But, far and away, our favourite route to find wine is to take a trip to the local wineshop, a retailer that specializes in wine, with a twinkle of passion in his or her eye. Our criteria for a great wineshop are:

Selection.
A good wineshop owner will go out of the way to bring in unique, intriguing bottles. He or she will constantly be sourcing new wines, with a passion to share these finds. A great wineshop does this and more, offering a great selection across all price ranges.

Staff.
Staff is easily the number one asset of a good wineshop. The staff has to not only be knowledgeable, but approachable as well. If you're not comfortable, move on, but when you find a shop with good employees, take advantage of their passion. They'll delight in offering an opinion.

Atmosphere.
Once we walked into a shop in downtown London where two pasty-faced old guys were sitting in the back, eating a morsel of cheese. They seemed oblivious to our entrance; we obviously didn't smell like money. Contrast this to the experience at a shop in downtown Calgary, where upon entering we were greeted and offered a taste from the bottle they had open, along with knowledgeable assistance when required.

collecting wine

have

on

hand

a

bottle

each of

red,

white,

and

bubbly

You should, at the very least, have on hand a bottle each of red, white, and bubbly. Just in case. If you do, then you are a wine collector. You probably won't believe us, but size doesn't matter, and this should never be the basis for judging wine competency. Having any wine lying around makes for good living, and accounts for a bona fide wine collection. Once this is recognized, you can decide how much effort to put into your collection, and what kind of collector you want to be.

types of collectors

Basic.
Granted, not everyone has the desire to invest significant time and monetary resources in wine. We're willing to accept this. All we ask is that the Basic Collector keep a few bottles on hand to assuage moments of spontaneity, incurred by themselves or their guests. Store the white and

sparkling in the fridge, the red wherever you please, and don't forget to replenish as necessary. Taking the basic collection to the next level would require the purchase of a dessert wine or port. This collection will serve you well for most everyday occasions.

Wine Investor.

To some, wine is pure investment. We're referring to those individuals who command wine portfolios—usually rather large collections of fine wines—as they would pork bellies or Microsoft stock. The thought brings a profound stench to our olfactory bulbs. In recent years, the Wine Investors have managed to raise some prices to such exorbitant and artificial levels that the average drinker's lips will never have a chance to touch a glass. The shame of it all is that some of these investor types do not even drink wine. Nothing short of scathing remarks shall be reserved for this type of collector. This is not to be confused, however, with investing *in* wine, a time-honoured tradition of saving bottles to be shared with loved ones, friends, and enemies alike.

Wine Lover.

We all have the potential. You don't even have to be romantic to be a Wine Lover, though the wine ought to help. Whatever your creed or motivation, the Lover collects wine for the pure enjoyment of future consumption. There are many types of Wine Lover, for example the *wine scenester*, label-conscious and varietal hip. Or, consider the *wine adventurer*, always on the make for something different. The *neoclassical wine lover* has theories on why she never tires of the tried and true, drinking Bordeaux and Chianti through and through.

you

don't

even

have

to be

romantic

to

be a

wine

lover

types of collections

"He who dies with the most toys wins," was a marketing credo making the rounds a few years ago. Without even debating the materialistic ideologies behind such a statement, when it comes to collecting wine, this is ill advice. No matter what type of wine collection you aspire to, does it make sense to maintain more than you can drink in a lifetime?

Horizontal.

The idea of this broad-based type of collection is to amass a worldly syndicate of wine in varied styles. A well-rounded collection would permit you to drink yourself around the world. The beginnings of a horizontal collection would be comprised of French Bordeaux and Burgundy, Chianti and Barolo from Italy, German Riesling, Spanish Rioja, and port from Portugal. Add Shiraz from Australia and New Zealand Sauvignon Blanc, pick up some Cab Sauv from Cali and a Pinot Gris from the Pacific Northwest. Find a Merlot from Chile, round it out with Argentine Malbec, and you have the makings of a classic representation of the important grape varieties.

Vertical.

Here the motto is "go deep." If you find yourself swept off your feet by a particular wine from a particular producer, why not see if previous or subsequent years are just as captivating? The idea behind vertical collections is to have different vintages of the same wine—stacked vertically if you want—allowing for comparative tasting. For starters, wines that have ageing potential, such as reds with good tannin structure, make good candidates.

a

well-rounded

collection

would

permit

you to

drink

yourself

around

the

world

Ad Hoc.

If depth and breadth are not your thing, just collect away and see what happens. The shotgun approach may not be traditional, but it makes for interesting evenings. A good grounding for Ad Hoc collections is tying an experience to each bottle. Even though it's one of those things that is difficult to quantify on a numerical scale, wine always tastes better when there's a story attached.

the new cellar

Admittedly, having a wine collection leads to questions of storage. How should wine be stored? How long does it last? What wines should you keep?

Why Age?
Contrary to popular belief, older is not necessarily better. The honest truth is that, give-or-take, 90 percent of wines produced today are ready to be drunk the moment they are purchased. This has given rise to the notion of "trunk ageing," the romantic process that occurs during the drive home from the wineshop. These wines will be great now, next week, six months from now... but there's no reason to hold onto them.

Of the remaining wine, ageing lets the wine develop in the bottle. A wondrous thing about wine is its ability to transform as it matures, turning into a completely different experience. As whites age they darken in colour, while reds lighten and the fruit and tannin structures mellow. An old wine is a completely different concept; like a well-produced music remix, it incorporates the original product into a new ideal, maintaining its integrity while adding new layers of enjoyment.

contrary

to

popular

belief,

older

is not

necessarily

better

Which Wines Age?

Though open to experimentation, it's generally accepted that reds age longer than whites. That said, particularly stodgy whites such as Sauternes, Riesling, and Chardonnay can show quite well into maturity. But reds are more durable due to the tannins in the wine that act as natural preservatives, slowly deconstructing into postmodern bliss over the years. Tradition has it that Cabernet-based wines last the longest, hence the status afforded often unaffordable Bordeaux. It's also important to consider the winemaking style. Even if the wine is a powerhouse red, if it has not been made with ageing in mind, it's not going to last.

Proper Storage.

If you've gone to the extent of investing in wine for the long run, it'd be sacrilege to not take proper care of it. Cellars, the traditional ten-feet-underground sort of thing, can be a little unwieldy. They may have been cool, say in Jane Austen's time, but attaining such an environment today could easily require immense financial investment, or moving, so we encourage creative cellar development.

Just remember that the enemies of wine remain heat, light, and movement. Extremes of these will leave you looking sour as you pull the cork on what has become vinegar.

Cellars, much like pets, should be an extension of their owners' personalities. (Also note that a well-chosen bottle of wine, much like a carefully selected dog, provides a good opportunity for singles to mingle.) Thankfully, technology has brought us nifty things like fridge-style cellar units, but under a bed is (literally) a handy place to keep wine too, as is the bottom of a closet, or seldom used corner of a loft. A current project of ours is the conversion

it's

generally

accepted

that

reds

age

longer

than

whites

of an old Frigidaire into a 48-bottle capacity storage unit, complete with chrome accents. It's going to be a dandy. Simply keep in mind the enemies of wine and proceed accordingly.

ideal cellar conditions

- constant temperature between 7°C–18°C (45°F–65°F), with 10°C (50°F) wine heaven
- 60% relative humidity
- on the dark side
- with as little movement as possible (some storage units sold in Japan come earthquake proof)
- bottles kept at an angle to keep the cork moist, so it does not dry, shrink, and subsequently let air in

what's in the *HALFAGLASS* cellar?

To be honest, we can't quite remember. Our wine currently rests in the basement of Kenji's grandfather's house, motivated by our need for mobility (but not fuelled by fear of commitment). As a precaution against immature consumption, we nailed the cases shut. This was some time ago.

serving
wine

chapter seven

Paris dripped with life; its streets packed with tourists, school children, and business men. As the warm day was turning into a cool autumn night, boys in the Marais paraded the sidewalk, flaunting their shiny haircuts past girls in woollen sweaters. I had a windbreaker on to keep the chill off and a baguette in my stomach. I found a Metro staircase and took it, passing through the turnstiles and into a tunnel where the air smelled like sandalwood and piss.

Le Verre Volé, in the 10ᵉ Arrondissement, was pointed out to me by a friend of a friend who lived in Paris and wrote for a newspaper. He wasn't an overly obsessed wine buff, but he knew his wines and knew where to get a good drink. I was grateful for his advice.

I surfaced from the Metro and back into the streets. The 10ᵉ Arrondissement was quite sedate compared to where I was staying. I turned down a darkening road, passing kids on dented caramel-coloured scooters and others resting in their cars, long cigarettes extending from their mouths. And down, down a ways I came to 67 rue de Lancry, the only door with life behind it on that barren street, the racket moving onto the sidewalk. Inside, there were tables of men with faces as red as the wine in the bottles that were stacked in columns up the wall. The ceiling rested on the necks of the best wine in France. And women

there

were

tables

of men

with

faces

as red

as the

wine

in the

bottles

100

wine

talked and laughed and nabbed cheeses off serving plates, ripped pieces of bread from loaves, and brought glasses to their ruby lips.

blowing

dust

off the

dark

bottle

A table of customers sat close to the kitchen, just under a speaker that blared ancient New Order hits. They were well through their third bottle when one of them stood up and requested an Hermitage, sending the waiter into the depths of the bar's cellar. He emerged shortly, blowing dust off the dark bottle that he carried in his right hand. In his left was a glass decanter.

Serving wine is a fantastic ritual, one that I never tire of observing. It could be done by a professional sommelier whose sweeping motions make me forget entirely place and time, but even at a local restaurant where I've ordered a couple of *tapas* and a bottle of the house wine, I still get all caught up.

The decanter, however, is a rarity. Or should I say, the calibre of wine I usually order doesn't call for one. And maybe the same held true for my neighbouring table, for as the wine was uncorked and dumped into the carafe, the party erupted into cheers and laughter.

Then suddenly, the man who ordered the wine leapt out of his chair, nearly sending it sprawling across the dented floor, and grabbed the decanter by its neck. He spun it in a wild circle, sending the wine inside sloshing, tracing purple spirals in the smoky light of the bar. He twisted his body to the music, holding the wine high above his head, shaking it mightily around and around.

By this time the entire bar's attention was turned to him, if not because of the raucous demonstration, then because of the deep aromas of Syrah bellowing out of the carafe.

The wine soon adequately oxygenated, the man upturned the decanter and let it slip into the waiting glasses. Drops fell onto the tabletop. I peered into the puddle they formed and saw my reflection in a million shades of red.

Kenji

opening the bottle

It's an all-too-familiar scene: your guests are seated around the table after introductions and general small talk. You've lit the candles, the silverware is polished to a mirror sheen, dinner is keeping warm in the oven, and the wine-glasses are set out. You bring the first bottle of wine out of the fridge and place it on the table: a Pinot Gris from Oregon, full of character, substantial, perfect pairing for the chowder appetizer. You cut off the foil from the neck of the bottle, turn the helical worm of the corkscrew into the centre of the cork, and you pull. You pull, but nothing happens. You grip the bottle between your thighs. You put it on the floor between your feet. Short of employing power tools, it seems, there is no way the cork will come free.

There is a corkscrew for everyone. Just as you have a favourite wine, you will have, or you will soon have, a favourite corkscrew. There are any number of types, from the classic and simple T-bar to the standard Waiter's Friend to the far more sophisticated Screwpull. And each has its advantages and disadvantages.

three easy steps

1. Cut the foil. Most corkscrews come with a functional foil cutter.
2. Twist the worm into the cork. Centred is best.
3. Pull.

types of corkscrews

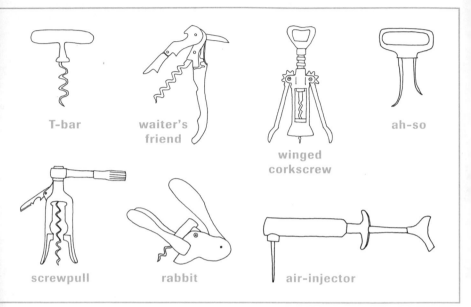

T-bar

waiter's friend

winged corkscrew

ah-so

screwpull

rabbit

air-injector

if you

haven't

been to

work out

your

forearms...

the t-bar

may not

be the

best

the T-bar

We like the T-bar. There's something to be said for its basic design: the worm spiralling beneath a form-follows-function handle. It doesn't get any more classic than this. That said, there are some ugly ones with handles made from pewter or driftwood, in the shape of a squirrel or a lesser appealing rodent. But there are also a number of slick-looking T-bars and they're not too pricy.

The problem with the T-bar, of course, is the effort required to remove the cork. Some corks these days are sealed substantially in the bottlenecks and, if you haven't been to work out your forearms of late, the T-bar may not be the best tool. Furthermore, with the advent of synthetic corks, which seem even more of a challenge to remove, you may find yourself cursing this corkscrew when all that is standing between you and a relaxing glass of wine is a stubborn stub of yellow plastic.

the waiter's friend

The beauty of the Waiter's Friend reverts back to the principle of one of the simple machines: the lever. This is really the ubiquitous corkscrew, and for good reason. A properly designed Waiter's Friend insures that no cork will be too long or too tight, with the supporting arm fast on the bottle neck and an easy stroke of the lever.

Though a great many Waiter's Friends have served their noble purpose well, the downside is, if designed poorly, they're not useful at all. That is, when they're equipped with a frustratingly short supporting arm that prevents the cork from coming clear out of the neck, their mechanical advantage is little better than that of a T-bar. The well-designed Waiter's Friend, however, is by far the corkscrew we use most.

the winged corkscrew

We swear that every household kitchen drawer must harbour a Winged Corkscrew, AKA the Butterfly, the bane of all cork-removal devices. There must have been some inexorable sales campaign in the late 1980s that drew such interest in this corkscrew. Maybe the same company that introduced us to abdominal machines was also commissioned to distribute propaganda about the merits of the Winged Corkscrew.

The great part is this: as you screw the worm into the cork, the wings fly up with the ratcheting mechanism. But the problem is this: as you push the wings down to draw

maybe

the same

company

that

introduced

us to

abdominal

machines

was also

commissioned

to distribute

propaganda

about the

merits

of the

winged

corkscrew

the cork, and then struggle mightily to disengage the last half inch of wood from the neck of the bottle, you might as well have reached into the fridge and cracked open a can of beer for all the effort it's taken to get a glass of wine.

crooked

butlers would

use this

corkscrew

to uncork

their

employer's

best bottles

of wine,

exchange

the wine

with cheap

plonk,

and

slip the

original cork

back in

the ah-so

Though being enamoured with this corkscrew's name ("Dishonest Butler" is its less interesting but more storied alias—more on this later), we are less confident of its usefulness. The idea is solid: the two prongs are slipped around the perimeter of the cork, and the Ah-So is twisted and pulled simultaneously to ease the cork out of the neck. There is no damage to the cork and for old corks that can crumble under a conventional corkscrew, the Ah-So is perfect.

However, it's not the easiest style to employ as the prongs have to be carefully inserted, and it takes some practice to see the cork actually comes out of the neck of the bottle. There's nothing wrong with practice, of course, even if it takes a number of bottles before you get it down. Just make sure you've got willing company who can drink the opened wine while you pull out the corks.

As for the "Dishonest Butler," legend has it that crooked butlers would use this corkscrew to uncork their employer's best bottles of wine, exchange the wine with cheap plonk, and slip the original cork back in, undamaged and unnoticed. They'd serve this wine when the party was well under way and guests couldn't tell the difference between a first growth Bordeaux and supermarket grape juice. As for the good stuff, we'd like to have been in on some of those butler parties.

the screwpull

Most certainly a pristine example of modernity, the Screwpull combines glossy design with tremendous ergonomic advantage. You simply wrap the plastic sheath around the bottleneck and, well, screw. Enough said.

the rabbit or similar

The Rabbit, along with similar incarnations, is a hand-held version of the bar-mounted, heavy-duty, high-volume corkscrew. For catering operations and busy restaurants, often there's a corkscrew attached to the bar that can systematically remove a cork in seconds. It's nothing short of impressive, and very practical for these environments.

The Rabbit, then, works on the same principle whereby you simply plunge the rotating worm into the cork via a handle, and the reverse operation neatly pulls the stopper from the bottle. But the Cadillac of corkscrews doesn't come without a Cadillac price tag. You can decide how much you need to spend to get a piece of wood out of the neck of a bottle.

air injection

A hollow needle is driven through the length of the cork and either air or compressed carbon dioxide from a canister is injected into the airspace within the wine bottle. This way, pressure is built up in the cavity until the seal gives and the cork pops out of the bottle.

It's debatable whether this is the culmination of modern technology applied to the corkscrew, or if the process is actually damaging to the wine. Either way, we suspect there's a less dramatic way to get a drink.

you

simply

wrap the

plastic

sheath

around

the

bottleneck

and,

well,

screw

decanting

Decanting is simply moving the wine from the bottle into another vessel. Of course, it's not always necessary to decant wine, and certainly the inability to do so should never stop you from drinking a bottle of wine. *Rappa-nomi*, a drinking style employed in modern Japan whereby the bottle is held to the lips and readily inverted, for example, does not imply decanting.

But if you have handy anything from a cradle decanter (an elaborate device that involves the incremental angling of the bottle by means of a threaded spool) to an old—but clean—water jug, both old and new wine can benefit from decanting.

old wine

If you let an older wine stand upright, over the course of a day you will likely be able to notice a collection of sediment forming at the bottom of the bottle. This is a natural result of the ageing process and of the lack of filtration in older wines. It's only been recently that producers have become keen on extensive filtering, a winery practice that guarantees a sediment-free wine (more on this later). So, sediment in these older wines is a result of lighter filtration or no filtration at all.

While sediment may taste a bit bitter or look unappetizing, there is no harm in gulping it back. But having to pick bits of crystallized tartrates and pigmented tannins from your teeth is generally not a smooth way to drink wine, so decanting becomes a useful tool. Let the wine sit in the upright bottle to allow the sediment to settle, and as you pour the wine into the decanter, carefully watch for the sediment and stop pouring just before it leaves the bottle.

just a bit of dirt

It is interesting to note that we have become so used to perfectly clear wine that many people mistakenly see the presence of sediment as a fault in the wine. Precipitation of sediment is a natural process and it has no ill effects on the wine. In fact, the bits may add a bit of flavour.

new wine

The reality of the market these days is that most of the wines on the shelves of your local wineshop are meant to be drunk today. And it is a rarity to find sediment in these new wines.

This status quo has come about primarily because large-volume producers have taken to strict filtering methods to ensure that a minimal amount of sediment, if any at all, can be detected in their wines. Regardless of whether you decant the wine or not, then, the liquid is perfectly clear in your glass with no muss or fuss.

So, while decanting new wine is not needed to remove sediment, it can be done to allow the wine to breathe. Though some debate still surrounds the issue, a great deal of new wine benefits from breathing. Breathing is simply the exposure of wine to oxygen so that the ensuing chemical effects allow its aromas and flavours to loosen up and become more apparent.

To be honest, just popping the cork and letting the bottle sit on the counter is a pretty ineffectual way to let a wine breathe; doing this, only a small surface area—in fact just the area of the bottleneck—is allowed to interact with air and not a lot of breathing takes place. Thus, decanting is the preferred option, as the agitation of the liquid permits good contact with oxygen.

Since with new wine it's unlikely that you'd have to watch to make sure sediment stays in the bottle, you can tip the bottle at a generous angle over the decanter and let the wine spill freely. If you wish, and aren't wearing your best whites, a few good swirls of the decanted wine never hurts.

Serve the wine immediately. Drink heartily.

types of decanters _____

just

as we

have to

endure the

likes of

battlefield

earth

and *ai,*

some

decanter

styles

should just

never have

been made

There are as many types of decanters as there are sci-fi flicks. And just as we have to endure the likes of *Battlefield Earth* and *AI*, so too some decanter styles should just never have been made.

But having said that, there are the classics that meld timelessness with practicality (think *The Fly*, *Blade Runner*), and it may be worth putting a bit of money into these. Pricier models are made of proper crystal and are recognizable by their weight (crystal contains lead) and delicate construction. Less expensive decanters are made of glass.

Both, however, should have a narrow neck to pour the wine into, and a wide base to allow for oxygen to reach a large surface area. The design should also allow you to swirl the wine in the decanter. The key, though, is air exposure, and as long as the decanter has some sort of width to it, it should be fine.

So go ahead and decant with confidence: there's nothing wrong with the designer decanter that matches your Arne Jacobsen chair that you curl up on to watch *2001: A Space Odyssey*. Just as there's nothing wrong with decanting your wine into an old—but clean—water jug.

serving temperature

An often-overlooked factor for complete wine enjoyment is serving temperature. The usual rhetoric suggests that white wines should be served chilled, and reds served at room temperature. In theory this is true, but practice more likely sees whites served straight out of the fridge and reds weathering a warm kitchen counter. As such, white wines are frequently served too cold, and oppositely, reds too warm.

Chilling a wine to typical fridge temperature (0°C–5°C [32°F–41°F]) works well to give you a crisp drink for the patio, but this can hide a white's most interesting characters. Pull your more complex white wines out of the fridge 20 minutes or so before dinner to serve them around 14°C (57°F).

Secondly, "room temperature" can be too vague for your fastidious reds. Without getting into deep debate about how you like your room temperature, we think reds are best served around 16°C (61°F). Too hot, and the volatility of the alcohol starts taking over; too cold, and the taste of the wine is all but lost, leaving a glassful of tannins.

Naturally, there are exceptions. Sweet white wine served colder (8°C [46°F]) keeps it from being too cloying. Sparkling, at a similar temperature, will prevent the bubbles from getting too overzealous. Try lighter reds at 12°C (53.5°F) for refreshment value.

So with this in mind, and thermometer at the ready, try chilling a bottle each of red and white, and drink them over the course of an evening, tasting them as they gradually come to ambient temperature.

pouring wine

Pouring wine is not one of the more rigorous areas of study within the topic of wine enjoyment, but it nevertheless deserves mention. It is, after all, the step separating wine in the bottle from wine in your glass.

It is always tasteful to hold the wine bottle by its widest part, the base, give a slow and steady pour, and a clever turn of the wrist to catch the drip as you right the bottle. Of course, we can't help liking the fellow we met in France who would grab the bottle by its neck with clenched fist and send the wine catapulting into our glasses, often onto the table in the process. The bottle would shake precariously, though it was never certain whether it was due to the weight imbalance or simply his convulsive love for the wine.

Tasting wine—assessing colour, smell, flavour, and feel—is always easier with less in your glass. Enough to swirl and get a good mouthful, but not so much that it becomes cumbersome. Drinking it, on the other hand, often works better with a good hearty pour. But whether you fill your glass half full or half empty is, well, up to you.

glasses

stemware shapes

bordeaux

burgundy

champagne

chardonnay

port

riesling

sherry

Glasses, or stemware as they are also known, are natural extensions of wine, serving as the vessels that bear the liquid before you toss it back into the next container, your stomach. As this is the case, literally any device that can contain wine will do, from industry standardized tasting glasses to designer crystal to the coffee mug with "I Love NY" emblazoned on the side that you received for your last birthday from your auntie.

Wine, in its natural environment, where it is nothing more special than the predecessor to coffee or tea in the course of a meal, can be served in basic glasses, *sans* stem. There's no reason the same glass can't be used for water, then wine, then coffee. In fact, there's something bohemian about drinking expensive Burgundy from a juice glass. And in a pinch, you could cut the bottom off an Evian bottle, or cup your hands together well.

But just as it is impossible to ignore the ubiquity of SUVs, we cannot disregard stemware. As with sport utility vehicles, stemware comes in all shapes and sizes, from the obviously useful to the downright ludicrous and, likewise, as much as we question the practicality of Excursions and Grand Cherokees, we admit these novelties have a distinct *raison d'être*.

To be sure, proper stemware has its place in wine appreciation. Much effort has been put into finding exactly the right shape of glass to bring out the best in a particular type of wine. Bordeaux glasses can be monstrous in size, red Burgundy glasses round like fishbowls, and champagne flutes narrow to preserve the wine's bubbles, or mousse.

For proper wine tasting, the glass should adhere to a few fundamentals. It should have a globular bowl made of glass for holding the liquid, a stem, and a base. The clarity

just

as

it is

impossible

to ignore

the

ubiquity

of SUVs,

we

cannot

disregard

stemware

of the glass allows you to properly see the colour of the wine. The stem allows you to hold the glass without changing the temperature of the wine with your hand. And the base offers stability, for the times when things may not be so stable. Adhering to these requirements, wineglasses range from the very basic IKEA genre to the more elegant, and less disposable, lead-crystal sorts, such as the likes of Riedel, the most prominent maker of high-end stemware.

To the wine aficionado, stemware is of prime importance. The glass must be crystal with a decent percentage of lead, it must have a stem of respectable length, and there must be the proper-shaped bowl for each different type of wine. Crystal can be made far thinner than conventional glass which, besides appearing more ornamental, is said to be less intrusive when observing the liquid. What's more, these glasses have a nearly undetectable coarseness to them so that, when swirled within, the wine remains suspended on the walls for a longer time. In turn, this gives a better perception of the aromas.

Red wineglasses are noticeably larger than those for white wine. The rationale here is that red wine is typically more complex and needs the additional surface area and volume to do it justice. And Burgundy glasses are commonly more obese than Bordeaux, with fans of the former arguing that the complexities in a Burgundy validate the extravagant size.

Riesling glasses can have a subtle lip at the opening, suggesting you ingest the (often) off-dry wine beyond the sweet sensory nerves at the tip of your tongue in order to distinguish its other attributes. Sherry glasses, or *copitas*, are more compact to funnel the aromas to your nose. Port glasses are not unlike a larger version of the copita.

red

wineglasses

are

noticeably

larger

than

those

for

white

wine

We've been to wine tastings where people have brought their own special tasting glass. They promenade into the room with a little box under their arm, dust off their beloved utensil that is usually some odd-looking abstraction of a regular glass, and banter loudly about their spot on the waiting list for a cult wine from California. And we've held overcrowded, impromptu wine parties where the latecomers have had to drink out of wide-mouth Mason jars. At least they're glass, we told them.

So when it comes right down to it, and there is wine to be drunk, it doesn't matter how much girth your bowl has or how long your stem. Use a glass, a clean glass if possible, and enjoy the wine that's in it.

coupes

Champagne was for a long time served in coupes: wider, rounder glasses, reportedly shaped after Marie Antoinette's left breast. Anatomy aside, how well the coupes preserve the mousse is something we'll let you get a handle on yourself.

leftovers

On the rare occasion that there is wine left over in the bottle, it is necessary to make sure it doesn't spoil. That is, some air contact can be beneficial for wine (one of the reasons for decanting), but beyond the duration of a sitting, lunch or dinner for example, further exposure to oxygen will strip the wine of its best aromas and flavours.

The longer the wine is left open, the more it will degrade. One day is tolerable, two is stretching it, and we don't recommend more than three. So what do you do with your leftovers? This question invokes endless debate, and solutions range from the simple to the ridiculously involved.

Of course, the quick and dirty is to put the cork back in the bottle and leave it on the counter. It's not a bad option if the romance has taken a turn for the better and you don't want to waste any time worrying about the rest of the wine. Unfortunately, re-corking the bottle leaves air inside and likely the wine won't taste the same the following day. But, you're probably not too concerned about this triviality anyhow.

You can re-cork and refrigerate. By cooling the wine in the fridge, you slow down the chemical reaction between the wine and the air, so the degeneration of the flavour is lessened. Not the perfect solution, but on your way to the bedroom, you might as well pop it in the icebox. Just remember to bring it back to the right temperature before you serve it the next day.

Vacuum pumps are a good method to save your wine. A rubber cork with a one-way valve is inserted into the neck of the bottle and a pump removes the air from inside. It's a painless, re-usable system, though be aware that it's not a perfect vacuum, so there will still be some compromise in aroma and flavour.

Wineries use inert gas such as argon to keep their wine from spoiling. The gas is heavier than air so it blankets the wine and doesn't react with the wine the way air does. The gas is also available to the consumer in more practical quantities, one can lasting for about one hundred applications. You simply spray the stuff into the bottle and leave it upright on the counter. But be cautious: some brands are

if

romance

is in

the

air and

passion

isn't

waiting for

anyone,

wine

preservation

is probably

the last

thing

on

your

mind

better than others; the worst ones seem to give the wine a pungent chemical flavour.

We've even seen sets of sealable decanters of varying sizes, so depending on how much wine is left, you can pour it into the appropriate-sized container, cap it, and be content with knowing there is the least amount of air remaining within the vessel. This is taking wine preservation to the extreme, but with the advent of extreme sports and extreme living, perhaps the time has come to explore extreme wine drinking.

Maybe the best solution, if you really do have wine left over in the bottle at the end of your meal, is to bring out a plate of cheese and some bread and keep going. But like we said, if romance is in the air and passion isn't waiting for anyone, wine preservation is probably the last thing on your mind. So just put a cork in it.

pump up the jam

These days, using a vacuum pump on an unfinished bottle of wine may be the most popular way to preserve it. Removing oxidative air from the bottle will keep the flavours intact, but is there a danger in over-pumping? Reports vary on the issue, though we've heard some claims of wine becoming flat after particularly enthusiastic pumping. Two or three strokes are adequate.

ordering
wine

chapter eight

ordering

"my

name's

hugo,

you

know,

like

the

boss"

"My name's Hugo, you know, like the Boss," he said with a grin as he extended his hand. The bartender's introduction caught me off guard, what with my limbs fatigued and my head muddled. I had spent the better part of the day traipsing through neighbourhoods of Buenos Aires, a fine city of sensual demeanour. It had been a full day, conducted mostly by foot under the watch of a late autumn sun that left me feeling sponge-like, counter to the cooling claims of the natural cotton fibre on my back. Tourist map in hand, I had explored the colourful homes along the portside streets of La Boca, too many of which were buried behind a tour bus façade. Later, from the lead of a lovely local, I had cavorted through the up-and-coming, fashionably funky boutiques of Pallermo, north of the city centre.

That evening, however, I was looking for a respite, and found it in a wineshop in the financial district of downtown BA. As these things usually go, I heard about the spot from someone who knew someone who was an associate of another. I was terribly underdressed for such a business-class affair. Of course, this being early 2001, the Argentine bankers had more pressing concerns than devaluing my unstylish ego.

The place itself was a marvel. All sheen and glass, in the aching stylish accord I had come to expect from

wine

Buenos Aires. Two stories, the place was nothing short of a wine oasis, with the ground floor housing a retail establishment and the belly a restaurant-cum-wine bar.

nothing

short

I scanned label after label of previously unknown wine, to the point that the possibilities seemed endless. So much wine, but never enough time; I was forced to focus. Malbec it would have to be, as it was the grape that for me symbolized Argentina's moody sensuality. Fortunately, I was informed that many of the shop's bottles were available to order by the glass downstairs.

of a

wine

oasis

Down the stairs I went and entered the bar, which was equally hip. I made my way to the counter in the back, where my new friend Hugo asked what I fancied. "When in Argentina drink Malbec," I decreed, and queried what he had on tap. Being a gent of temperance, I recognized partaking in all the wines, even by the glass, would leave me in a sorrier state than the protagonist in a tango. As a solution, I inquired into the possibility of ordering a flight of Malbecs. "No problem," answered Hugo, and in no time the boss had recommended five.

The wines literally were on draught, the open bottles housed behind a plate of glass, encased in a stainless steel, wood-trimmed box, with taps fit snug to the bottle tops. A digital read-out on the display panel informed that the cabinet was temperature-controlled. The sanity of it all may be questioned, but there was no denying the unit was impressive.

Hugo flipped the appropriate levers for my five bottles, eyeballing a two-ounce pour into each glass. He placed the five glasses in front of me, then abruptly motioned for me to wait. In no time he produced five new glasses, each big enough to house a goldfish, the kind of crystal that could physically hold an entire bottle's worth of wine, giving new dimension to the doctor's recommendation of "a glass of wine a day." The bartender then explained that the normal serving glasses would not suffice, since I was a visitor to Argentina and about to drink wines that represented the spirit of his country. At least I think that's what he said—admittedly, my Spanish is not fluent. In any event, it was the kind of patriotism I could appreciate.

I relaxed on my stool and, seeing that I was alone, took out my notebook to record my reflections on the day and

would

leave

me in

a sorrier

state

than

the

protagonist

in a

tango

the wine. Hugo seemed to think it was great that I was going to take notes on his wines, and he brought me bowls of sun-dried olives and breadsticks. Felt mighty fine as I settled into my flight, the best $15 I've ever spent on wine.

the restaurant scene

The awful truth is that not enough people order wine when dining out at restaurants. Too often, the "dining" is taken literally, to the detriment of the drinking. If you've come to enjoy and expect the pleasures derived from the wine-and-food marriage, it'd be a shame to opt out of the fun of ordering wine.

Of course, this assumes the ordering process is consistently pleasurable, which is far from true. Sure, we've heard all the excuses before, mostly variations on the themes of fear, price, selection, and societal pressures. Sadly, these concerns are often founded.

On the other hand, many diners refuse to accept that ordering wine at a restaurant is different from cracking a bottle at home. In order to have our wine and drink it too, we will put aside grievances and seek to mitigate a harmonious union between consumer and restaurateur.

It's true: wine costs more in a restaurant. If you went to the grocery store and bought the ingredients used in the dishes at your favourite eatery, you'd find a price discrepancy there as well. The markup on the wine, like the markup on the food, covers staff costs, rent, inventory, marketing, and any other items that keep the restaurant a going concern.

The difference is one of perceived labour. It's much easier to rationalize the work put into food prep and presentation, compared with the labour-to-cost ratio of pulling a cork and pouring. So, what's a fair markup? Well, it remains subjective. Just as some are comfortable shopping at the GAP, others would only be seen in Banana. Both may sell chinos and wholesome simple style, but nonetheless the pricing differs dramatically. So many factors, from ambience to occasion to location, are at play. On wine, from our experience, a markup of 100% is average.

a simple economic study of restaurant wine prices

Given a current price [P1] a restaurant sells a quantity [Q1] of wine, generating actual revenue of R1 = P1 x Q1. What if, perhaps by chance or throw-caution-to-the-wind determination, the restaurant were to lower the price to [P2], perhaps thereby increasing the quantity sold to [Q2], to realize potentially higher revenues of R2 = P2 x Q2, where R2 > R1?

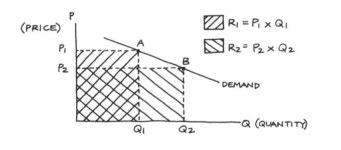

selection

It makes sense—from everyone's perspective—that a restaurant should strive to provide a unique selection of wines. Since you're paying more, this would be a perfect opportunity to try a fun, new bottle. Restaurants often have access to bottles not normally found on retailer's shelves, so if they care about wine, they will go out of their way to offer some surprises. And assuming they care about food and wine, some thought will have been made to select wines that complement their dishes.

Also to note is the "by the glass" selection. Offering wines by the glass is no easy task, as once the bottle is opened, wine has a short lifespan. A wide array is usually a good indication of a restaurant with a reputation for wine, one with brisk wine sales. A restaurant's wine list is the metaphorical eye into the window of its soul.

service

You should also be privy to good wine service. Knowledgeable staff is a bonus, but we're not talking white gloves and *tastevins*. We think great service, like successful day trading, is having substantial capacities of anticipation—to know how much service is just enough. Some tables may desire the full ritual, pop, and circumstance; others may simply want the cork out and the bottle on the table, post haste. Both have their place, and it's the staff's job to figure out the necessary level of attention.

the role of the sommelier

You've probably seen the word; more than likely you wonder how to say it. It's *som-mill-lee-eh* and it's French for, more or less, a specialized wine waiter. Better high-end eateries often employ a sommelier, with job details that can incorporate everything wine related, such as ensuring proper wine service, offering advice on wine *when requested*, managing the restaurant's cellar, and at times buying the restaurant's wines. Most countries have recognized sommelier education programmes that involve rigorous training that is taken quite seriously. A true sommelier has no qualms about being called a wine geek, and their opinions are worth soliciting when you find one in a restaurant.

navigating the wine menu

Hand people a wine list in a restaurant and they'll: instantly form nervous beads of sweat across their brow; promptly hand it to someone else; order a beer.

In reality, wine lists are nothing to be afraid of, unless they're bound in leather and come wheeled to the table on a dolly. Those tomes still scare the wits out of us. But most restaurants have recognized the importance of having concise wine menus that are easy to find a way around. That said, even if the list runs to only one page, if it causes confusion, it has been written incorrectly.

the step-by-step ordering guide

The trick is to get your bearings, put everything in context, reduce your options, and don't look back. Advice to follow for love as well.

Determine how the list is organized.
Briefly scoping the wines should give you an idea of how the list is organized. Common methods include referencing by country or region, perhaps by wine type, maybe by price, or perchance a cross-reference of these.

Put things in context.
How much do you want to spend? Who are you dining with? What are they eating? How many bottles will be ordered? The answers to these questions are crucial for your wine selection.

Reduce your options.
It's the same strategy as is employed on multiple-choice exams. If you know there are wines you won't be ordering, remove them as options. Is there a wine you know you don't like? Or one that will not work with the food? Bottles that are out of your budget?

Make a selection.
Pat yourself on the back. Revel in the fawning compliments on your wine expertise. Then tip us accordingly.

the future of wine lists

The wine list, just like every other facet of modern-day life, is subject to trends. We can take them or leave them, but there are some concepts that are showing up on many a fashionable establishment's list. Some restaurants now use "one price" wine lists, which takes the price factor out of the selection process. More eateries seem to be writing descriptions of their wines which, when done correctly, are helpful tools. Hip haunts sometimes organize their lists according to unorthodox style categories, such as "fresh and fruity" or "big and bold." Some restaurants have decided to make a suggestion of a wine to pair with a particular dish. This shows a level of commitment to both food and wine, and is an encouraging sign.

the ritual

Recently, there has been concern over a lack of rituals in North American culture. Short of going to the mall or watching television, a drought of ritualized behaviour is said to be leading to incoherent community, creating an individualized culture of "me." (Give us a glass of wine and we'll discuss the topic at length.) However, there is one ritual we'll gladly say is alive and well, not only in North America, but the world over. The ritual is the ceremonious, if somewhat curious, serving of a bottle of wine at the table. And in some Far Side alternative, animal-run universe, we're sure the cows delight in watching this ceremony unfold on their roles-reversed Nature Channel.

the presentation

The server or sommelier will bring the selected bottle to the table and present it to the host, the person who ordered the wine. The point here is to determine, perhaps obviously, that the wine is the one you ordered. Not so obvious may be remembering to double check that the vintage corresponds with the one on the wine list, if such a thing concerns you. Also, it's helpful to feel the bottle, to make sure it's at the right serving temperature. You do, after all, want the wine to be appropriately chilled (or not).

the cork

Assuming a match is made, the cork will be relieved from the bottle. Somewhere, sometime, somehow (we have a feeling Hollywood played a part) popular fashion saw fit to begin sniffing the cork. This actually serves little purpose as the cork smells like wood and you're more concerned with what's in the bottle. Cork sniffing is an attempt to smell a faulty wine, but this is best achieved in the next step. Instead, to really impress your compatriots, squeeze the cork and explain you're checking for a cork that responds with gentle resiliency, not one that's rock hard or flabby, which are possible signs of cork failure. It also doesn't hurt to look at the cork. If wine has seeped to the very top, it could indicate that air has penetrated into the bottle.

the judgement

After receiving the cork, a small amount of wine will be poured into the host's glass. Here, the real fun begins and you get to employ your sensory evaluation skills. The first task is to look at the wine. Murkiness or an off-putting colour should have alarm bells ringing. Next, give a sniff. By this point you'll most likely have determined if the wine is off, but a taste will reaffirm your suspicions. If all smells in order, then continue to the next step.

the pour

Assuming the wine passes muster, give the server a thumbs-up, nod of the head, jive handshake, or whatever other hip gesture is the parlance of the day. The wine will now be poured around the table, tradition dictating the server work clockwise from the guest seated next to the host, ladies first. An exception would be any guest of honour who is present, as they always get served first. Alternatively, tradition be damned, pour the wine yourself and be done with it.

sending wine back

When is it appropriate to send a wine back? It is your market-given consumer right to send back a wine which is faulty, or one that is not the same as listed on the menu. It is not reasonable to refuse a wine on the grounds that it tastes different from what you expected. A restaurant should not be held accountable for subjective sentiment.

wine ordering scenarios

The dim sum business lunch.
Much to the detriment of capitalist affairs, wine with lunch seems somewhat of a faux pas these days. Before the global community becomes boringly homogenized, we offer the following advice: considering the situation and acknowledging the challenge of matching the complex, varied flavours of dim sum, we would search the wine list for a sparkling wine (champagne if it's an important affair).

Business dinner at the new hot spot.
Here we have potential for a tense situation, but thankfully wine has been known to be a business lubricant. The odds are you're looking to impress, so this is one occasion when we'd stick with what we know and order something familiar. If the wine list offers no such choices, play it safe with the classics, such as Bordeaux, Barolo, or California Cabernet Sauvignon. These are wines Gordon Gekko would drink, even off Wall Street.

With your friends at a casual restaurant.
Allow us the assumption that not everyone will be as into wine as you. Keep it simple. For red, Australian Shiraz or Chilean Merlot is a usual crowd-pleaser; while in white, Chardonnay is never second-guessed. Or, if you see something you fancy on the wine list, go for it. If they're real friends, they'll support your wine interest.

wine ordering scenarios *continued*

First date at the romantic french restaurant.
Face it, France still holds court when it comes to romance. A legacy of fine wine, rich sauces, and Serge Gainsbourg: they all scream "lovin'." First dates are nerve-wracking. Beaujolais is the obvious choice (assuming your date drinks red). Fruity but robust enough to demand attention, it's a wine that, like a first date, does not require serious commitment. For the ultimate in romantic speculation, seek one out from Saint Amour, a tiny Appellation in the heart of Beaujolais with a name so perfect it hurts.

At the steakhouse with the wine expert.
There may come a time when you find yourself out dining with a known wine snob. With these types, two strategies emerge. First, there's the option to flatter the snob's sensibilities and ask them to order a bottle. Alternatively, call the restaurant in advance, inquire about the list, and have them make a recommendation. Slightly devious, but it will save you the hassle.

Also, make sure you get an impressive nugget of wine wisdom to drop while you order the wine. For example, "Well, we must have the '97 Château So and So because that year they installed and began crushing with their new bladder press, and the gentler process is evident in the smoother tannin structure." Smooth indeed.

wine making

wine

The decision to make wine from Pinot Noir grapes came mostly from my Uncle Bill. He had been making wine for years, sometimes red wine, sometimes white. He'd made everything from Merlot to Chenin Blanc. But one of his favourites was Pinot Noir.

Pinot Noir is a finicky wine. First off, the grapes are delicate and difficult to grow well. Secondly, it takes considerable experience to make a good wine from Pinot Noir, as the wine can come out dull if not handled in the right way. But my uncle, in a way that was as stubborn as a Pinot Noir grape, would not agree to help with any other variety.

So looking for quality grapes, I phoned around and located a reputable grower in the Okanagan Valley who agreed to sell a thousand pounds of the grape from his vineyard. "Cadillac grapes," he said, "I only grow Cadillac grapes." As for the requisite winemaking experience, I was relying on Uncle Bill.

"i
only
grow
cadillac
grapes"

In a rented panel van I left the city at 10 p.m., manoeuvring the bulky mass onto the highway and picking up speed until the empty garbage cans in the back shuddered with every bump on the road. Large oncoming trucks, making their way to the city, passed me quickly and the van shimmied in the draft.

making

air

smelling

like

greasy

eggs and

diesel

I arrived at a gas station close to the vineyard just as the sun was crawling over the hills that lined the valley. Huge rigs were parked in the lot and I could see the drivers having breakfast in the diner. It was cold in spite of the warming sunrise, and my breath made balloons of steam. I was exhausted from the drive so I laid a sleeping bag over the metal floor and slept.

I woke up to truck noises and air smelling like greasy eggs and diesel. The sun was making a dent in the freezing air.

Ron, the grape grower, met me as I drove onto his property. His vineyard spread for acres over an area sloping beneath the main road, precise rows of vines laid north-south to catch the best light. Irrigation posts stood evenly throughout each row, and propellers towered 10 metres (30 feet) over the vineyard. When I arrived, it sounded like all hell was breaking loose. The sprinklers were fanning the vineyard with jets of water, bird canons sent a periodic crack through the air, and the whop-whop-whop of the overhead windmills drowned out any other sound. "To prevent frost damage to the vines," yelled Ron, engulfing my hand in his, nearly shaking it off my arm. The water would coat the vines and bear the cold, while warm air was circulated downwards onto the vineyard.

I pulled the van back on the highway just after noon with the garbage cans full of Pinot Noir. Heavier now, the van did not quiver as it had before.

Uncle Bill was waiting when I got back to the city. I hobbled into his backyard, still stiff from the drive. A grape crusher, nothing less than ancient with its gnarly teeth and manual crank, sat waiting as well.

"Shall we get crushing, then?" asked Bill, the excitement in his eyes luminous in the dusk. We unloaded the grapes, placed the crusher over an empty can, and with no machine to de-stem the clusters of Pinot Noir, stood picking each grape from its assemblage.

We finished well past midnight. Tubs of grape juice lined the back porch and grape stems were scattered around our feet.

As I was cleaning up, moving the emptied garbage cans, rinsing the crusher, I paused briefly, looking across at the tubs brimming with the juice of the Pinot Noir grapes—

"shall

we get

crushing,

then?"

asked

bill, the

excitement

in his

eyes

luminous

in the

dusk

dark and inky in the guileless light of a halogen bulb. Uncle Bill was securing lids on the tubs, one by one, which would stay until the next day when we'd drop in the yeast to start the fermentation. He stopped momentarily and dipped two fingers into the grape juice, bringing them to his lips. The old flannel shirt covering his tall frame, green like the Okanagan vineyards, was smeared black from the skins of the Pinot Noir.

Kuji

red, white, and pink

Red wine is a result of red grapes (or black grapes, as they're often called after the colour of their skin) and white wine is a result of white grapes (that aren't really white). White wine can be a result of red grapes, but we haven't yet come across a red wine that's a result of white grapes.

It all comes down to the skins. So when the grapes are crushed or pressed, the skins of the black grapes are generally left to mix with the fermenting juice, literally dying the liquid various shades of red. The intensity of colour depends on the type of grape and time "on skins." Cabernet Sauvignon makes a dark wine, a heavy claret, whereas Pinot Noir is less severe and has a colour closer to cherry Jell-O. As an aside, tannins come mostly from the skins of grapes. Red wines have tannins.

White grapes, however, are pressed, then the juice is usually separated from the skins and fermented on its own. The colour of the wine is the same colour as the juice, and ends up in the bottle as a clear, vivid liquid in varying shades of yellow, from straw to gold to that of bruised lemons.

Then there's pink wine, or what's more commonly known as rosé. Rosé is made from black grapes, but the

pinot noir is less severe and has a colour closer to cherry jell-o

grape skins don't spend the whole time with the juice: less skin contact than a red wine, more skin contact than a proper first date. Rarer versions of pink wine are simply red and white mixed.

As for white wine made from black grapes? Champagne is made from Chardonnay, Pinot Meunier, and Pinot Noir, the latter two being black.

what's white zin?

White Zinfandel, the quintessential American pink wine, was first introduced in the 1980s. Its easygoing, uncomplicated, sweet style took the U.S. by storm, and even today one in every ten bottles opened in the country is the California blush.

Is it good? Though frowned upon by the wine "experts" as a syrupy simpleton, a Cali winemaker once told us white Zin is his hardest wine to make, what with the challenge of getting it perfectly pink year after year. White Zin's fruitiness is fine with cream sauces or pork dishes.

the magic formula

The Magic Formula, the formula for making wine, is
Sugar + Yeast = Alcohol + CO_2 + Heat.
Understanding where wine comes from—that is, the chemical conception of wine—gives insight into why wine is wine, why good wine is good, and, conversely, where bad wine went wrong. Though we won't purport to know why AC/DC still gets radio play or why goth refuses to die, there is a reason why you pour a glass of Merlot and it's as smooth as a car salesman's banter or as volatile as his polyester suit.

From the time grapes are picked off vines to bottling and shipping, any number of opportunities exist for highlighting the personality of the wine. So, while the Formula can appear simplistic, the astute winemaker is aware of where to interject. By optimizing the calibre of the grapes in the vineyard during the processes of pruning the vines and harvesting, or by tuning the wine via techniques in the winery such as secondary fermentation and oak storage, the winemaker can tweak a wine, within the framework of the Magic Formula.

Though it's not imperative to have a complete grasp of the subtle details of winemaking, it is certainly beneficial to have a general one, in order to know why your wine tastes the way it does.

the grapes

Sugar comes from the grapes. Buds appear on the vine in March (September in the southern hemisphere), and reach veraison, or the ripening stage, in August (February) when the acids that have built up in the berry begin to change into sugar. Just as any fruit has more or less sugar depending on its ripeness, grapes will have higher concentrations the longer they've been in the sun.

Along the way, the vines proliferate as Mother Nature, via photosynthesis, does her thing. To concentrate the vine's energy on the grapes, the zealous, leafy shoots are pruned back to a minimum, and the remainder is positioned to gain the most sunlight exposure from the least amount of foliage. Focusing the vine's development on the grapes and not the leaves means better-tasting fruit.

A single vine will produce some forty bunches of grapes and as many as thirty bunches of these may be cut off to concentrate efforts into what's left hanging on the vine. Again, this means better-tasting grapes. Older vines are also an asset. With maturity on their side, they no longer generate fruit with the fervour the UK breeds boy-bands; rather, the vines yield small quantities of good grapes. Wine doesn't benefit from all the excess.

Unless, of course, you're the one selling the grapes. Or growing the grapes and making the wine. In this case, cutting bunches of grapes off the vine is like watching money spiral down the proverbial toilet, and this gives rise to the endless tug-of-war between quality and quantity.

In some areas, namely France, regulations exist to prevent châteaux from this temptation of over-cropping. And other regions have their own respective quality regulations. But, as regulation rears its familiar head, loopholes are never far behind and many wineries know them all too well. So who can you trust? The surest strategy is to get familiar with a few different wineries of a region and see for yourself who is committed to making good wine. Trust your tongue.

Grape growers partially determine when the fruit will be harvested by examining the sugar levels of the grapes using a refractometer (a tool that lets light refract through grape juice) that measures in degrees Brix (or Baumé). The higher the Brix, the riper the fruit.

The flavour intensity of the grapes is the other facet the grower will consider when deciding when to pick the fruit off the vine. A juicy grape will make a juicy wine.

The conundrum here is that Brix is measurable, flavour intensity is not. It's one thing for a grape grower to write down a number and decide to harvest, it's another for them to put a berry in their mouth to make the decision. Going by the book does not always produce the best wine, but to do otherwise requires far more experience. The best growers, therefore, have a handle on both.

the

higher

the

brix,

the

riper

the

fruit

the yeast

Yeast is the organism that does all the work. Lifetimes have been spent researching yeast to find the best match for grapes, and the study is ongoing. The magic of yeast, however, is its ability to convert sugar into alcohol. And, by adding yeast to sweet grape juice, not only is alcohol rendered, but the basic flavours of the juice are turned into the complex flavours found in wine. This is the fermentation process.

Grape juice is dumped into vats—wood or concrete vats traditionally, but stainless steel these days—and yeast is added. The particular strain of yeast to add, the temperature of the fermentation (modern tanks are fitted with cooling jackets), and length of fermentation are variables decided by the winemaker.

the alcohol

The fermentation process yields alcohol. How much alcohol, or the percentage by volume as is the common labelling system (for instance, 12.5% al./vol.), is determined by how much sugar was in the grapes. A higher sugar level means a potentially higher alcohol level.

A general rule is the higher the alcohol level, the fuller-bodied the wine. The reason for this is that more alcohol in the wine means the fruit had more sugar when it was picked. This higher sugar level, or Brix, means the fruit was riper and more flavourful, leading to wine that is similarly appetizing.

But rules are made to be broken and we'd be lying if we suggested this rule is any exception. Like everything else these days, be it your workout regime or your mutual fund portfolio, wine needs balance. Sure, it's one thing to make a wine from super-ripe grapes verging on 14 and 15 percent alcohol (the high end of the spectrum for table wine), but if it's way out of whack, with no flavour to balance the alcohol so that all you taste is bitterness, it's not a great wine. It's probably not even a good wine.

In an opposite scenario, if the grapes haven't ripened enough and the sugar content is low, the alcohol level will be low. The wine won't be bitter with excessive alcohol, but excessive acidity from the unripe grapes will mean a harshly acidic wine. Again, poor balance.

Granted, grape growers and winemakers don't have an easy task. For example, Zinfandel, an American mainstay, has a notoriously high alcohol level as the grapes can ripen to some serious Brix. As such, the risk of a bitter Zinfandel is ever present. However, with proper attention from conscientious wineries, these can be lush, fruity, full-bodied wines that you'd never guess were upwards of 15 percent alcohol by volume. Balance is the key.

an explosion of ripe plums and chocolate

the rest

To finish looking at the Formula, carbon dioxide is a by-product that creates a protective blanket over the wine while it is fermenting. Heat is a result of the sugar-yeast reaction and is often regulated.

So when you sit down and open a bottle of Merlot, make sure it's one that tastes like an explosion of ripe plums and chocolate (good grapes, skilled winemaker), and not one that tastes like someone added food colouring to dish water (underripe grapes, poor fermentation).

crush on grapes

Yes, people used to crush grapes with their feet. They'd stand in a circular tub and dance on the fruit, and the juice would be released and collected for wine. Feet were seen as the optimum way to crush grapes, being far gentler than machines and soft enough not to squash the pips and stems, the parts of the grape cluster that contain the tannic chemicals that make a wine astringent.

Feet aren't used so much these days. Mechanical presses, often either a threaded horizontal press or a bladder press, are the norm. They do a pretty good job, though they're not as fun to watch.

malolactic fermentation

All wine goes through the first fermentation, the Magic Formula, but red wines, and some whites, undergo a secondary fermentation: malolactic.

Malolactic fermentation is the conversion of malic acid (think tart green apples) to lactic acid (think soft milk). This is the process that removes the astringency of an acidic wine and makes it smooth and easy on the palate.

Not all wines are subjected to this secondary fermentation. For it to occur, the wine needs to be at a temperature that cooler environments don't often reach, so cool-climate wines like Sauvignon Blanc and Gewürztraminer remain crisp and tart with malic acid. Red wines, and whites such as Chardonnay, however, are traditionally made in warmer climates and naturally undergo the fermentation that creates the softer lactic acid.

That said, these days winemakers are able to control malolactic, and hence can use it as another device to add style to a wine. If they want a big, buttery Chardonnay, M-L, as it's affectionately known, gets the green light. But

malolactic

fermentation

is the

conversion

of malic

acid

to

lactic

acid

if a winemaker wants to buck the trend and make a sharp, snappy Chard, he or she will probably forgo malolactic fermentation.

oak

The role of oak is twofold. On one hand, oak barrels are a really good way to store wine, which was their original purpose. On the other hand, oak barrels change the flavour of the wine they store. This observation has led to using oak barrels as a stylistic instrument.

So way back when it was common to gather around a dinner spread of hogs cooked on spits over open fires and drink from brimming goblets, and wine was stored in oak barrels somewhere up in the rafters. No one really cared that the wine had, more or less, a flavour of wood.

Then, along the way, someone figured that the oak barrels, besides being good containers, made the wine taste like oak. And that the taste of oak wasn't half bad. The other bright observation was that the oak barrels, while they contained the liquid very well, allowed for the slightest transaction of air. And while too much air contact will oxidize a wine (turn it into vinegar), the amount permitted by the porous wood is just enough to mature the wine nicely.

Now, it should be mentioned that there are two main kinds of oak barrels: French and American. Commonly, wine labels and wine write-ups will talk about, "aged nine months in new American oak" and, "matured in French *barriques* (barrels)." What's the difference? The French like to split their oak trees along the grain to make their barrels, resulting in less vanilla flavour making its way into the wine. The Americans, however, prefer to cut the wood in spite of the grain, giving a stronger seasoning.

Which is better? Patriotism aside, it all depends on how you like your wine. Stronger oak aromas and flavours are related to the length of time the wine has spent in the barrels, the age of the barrels (newer barrels = more flavour), and the type of barrels: French or American.

Of course, not all wine responds well to oak. Many white wines, and a sample of reds, taste better simply fresh and fruity without the oak flavour and without the barrel maturation. Common examples are Rieslings and Gewürztraminers.

A less romantic, albeit very realistic, point is that oak barrels are expensive. There is no denying that a large cost related to winemaking is the purchasing of the barrels. They range from about US $300 for American to over $600 for French, and a winery making 2500 cases of a wine can add some $2 onto the cost of a bottle by opting for barrels. But not to fear, progress is cousin to efficiency is cousin to quick and dirty winemaking, and often wineries will use oak chips, oak staves, two-by-fours, or other oak "technologies" mixed along with the wine in the fermentation vats. This gives the impression of oak without the exorbitant cost.

So these days, when you're more likely to gather around the Flame King gas grill BBQing portobello caps and drinking from plastic cups than you are to watch a hog rotating on a spit, know the vanilla aroma in your Chardonnay and the smoky flavour in your Shiraz are there for a reason.

know

the

vanilla

aroma

in your

chardonnay

and the

smoky

flavour

in your

shiraz

are there

for a

reason

style

Who can forget the classic bands of the 1980s? Duran Duran, Soft Cell, OMD, Eurythmics. Full-on classics in our books. No doubt they were radical and choice, awesome and gnarly. But even Quincy Jones, as he lowers the needle onto a worn copy of "Thriller," may very well admit the 1980s were all about the production studio, with its synthesizers and drum machines. Technology ruled the decade.

But we digress. As we have just explored, to get from what's in the vineyard to what's in the bottle, a series of production steps have to occur, generally at the hands of the winemaker. Much like Mr. Jones did with music, the winemaker can push and pull, tweak and twist, to create a wine that fits his or her vision. There are any number of controllable variables at their dispense. Or, the winemaker's philosophy may lie in the notion of *terroir*, and he or she may opt to intervene on a minimal level.

Terroir [tehr WAHR] is the character the vineyard and its environs give the wine. Local climate, slope and orientation of the land, and soil type are a few aspects that have a final effect on the wine. If a wine were entirely unplugged (in the MTV sense of the word), you would taste the terroir and nothing else.

It's not ours to say that one philosophy is better than the other. A wine demonstrating lots of terroir can illustrate where it originated from, with layers of distinctive character, but the same wine can be off-putting if you don't particularly care for the flavour of that particular region. Conversely, a wine completely devoid of terroir can be simply an over-the-top rush of velvety zest, but exactly the well-made, dependable wine you're looking for.

who can

forget the

classic

bands

of the

1980s?

duran

duran,

soft

cell,

omd,

eurythmics

What we're saying is, we used to listen to hours of raw, emotion-driven, hard-hittin' punk rock. Punk from guys like Ramone and Rotten who sang about how it really was. But when all was said and done, there was nothing like kicking back to the steadfast key-tar licks and drum rhythms of "Every Breath You Take" and "Charlotte Sometimes." On audiotape, of course.

wine to pair with granola

you

grew

out your

feathered

hair and

traded

your

pink

polo

for

plaid

flannel

Alas, the "me" decade had to come to an end. And about the same time as your tape deck started to go on the blink, you grew out your feathered hair and traded your pink Polo for plaid flannel. You made your first organic lentil and carrot soup.

Since then, the organic sections of supermarkets have multiplied faster than Starbucks in the suburbs. It wasn't too long ago when we had to travel to the city to get a fancy latte and to a farm to get organic produce. The beauty of this day and age is we can get both, a caffeine fix and natural fruits and vegetables, from stores within spitting distance of each other.

But what wine do you drink with the certified organic, ready-to-serve, pre-tossed salad? Or the grain-fed free-range chicken?

After so carefully matching the flavours of the food to the wine, it would be downright hypocritical to consider a sulphite-ridden, over-processed wine made from pesticide-saturated grapes. The solution? Organic wine, of course.

True chemical-free wine is wine that has no traces of sulphites, the common preservative, in the bottle. However, the reality of such truly "pure" wine is it is very susceptible to spoilage. Completely devoid of sulphites, the wine is extremely volatile, so that during transport and storage there exists a significant risk of the wine developing off flavours. Besides, sulphites in small amounts are naturally occurring and are removed completely only by a deliberate extraction process that is not a common practice, even for organic wineries.

So, unless you have a severe allergy to sulphites (the allergy exists, but is rare and often is only triggered by excessive amounts), it may be advisable to concede the existence of a minimal amount. Regulations exist in the U.S. and the European Union (more stringent in the latter) to certify organic wine with the provisions that it has been made from organic produce and the sulphite addition is below a defined level.

As for the grapes, to grow them organically requires more diligence than otherwise, as only natural fertilizers and pest controls are allowed. However, consumer demand for organic produce is certainly making necessary resources more available to farmers.

While some North American wineries and others from the New World have only recently been jumping on the organic bandwagon, many European winemakers have been pursuing this avenue for a few decades. Often the labels won't explicitly say that the wine is organic, but with a bit of research, or by asking your friendly neighbourhood wineshop, you can figure out who these wineries are.

However, much hesitation revolves around organic wines. And, to a certain extent, the caution is warranted. To be sure, with fewer controls such as insecticides in the vineyard, and more susceptibility to spoilage due to lack of sulphite addition, the wineries have a harder time guaranteeing the consistency of their wine. If the weather doesn't quite co-operate one year, or there's an emergence of damaging pests, the wine may not be up to snuff. It may not achieve its usual accolades and consumers may respond in kind.

On the other hand, even though your cappuccino has the same kind of coffee, the same amount of milk, and the same frothy blanket every time you order it, it doesn't mean your wine has to follow suit. There certainly lies an element

there

certainly

lies

an

element

of

romance

and

mystery

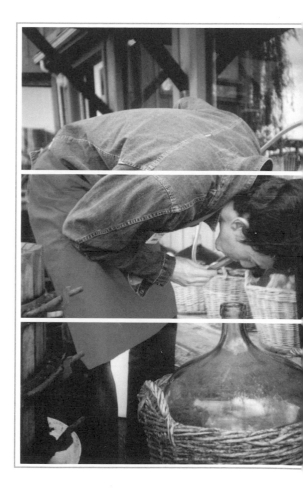

of romance and mystery, not to mention an opportunity to understand more about wine, in opening a bottle that is not going to taste the same every time.

Are they decent wines? Yes. Will they fly off the shelf like flabby Chardonnay in the discount bin? Questionable. But give them a try; they're good for you after all.

biodynamics

Biodynamic is organic to the next level. It still uses the basic organic principles, but in addition to excluding chemical fertilizers and such, it conceives the vineyard as a self-sufficient ecosystem. All very practical, you may think, but the hardcore biodynamicists believe their plants will thrive if planted, pruned, and harvested in accordance with the lunar cycle. They also believe they must indoctrinate the land with a cow's horn filled with manure, buried in the ground. Wacky, sure, but it's probably the most TLC any vineyard can see.

the old world

the old

to tell

the

truth,

it had

never

occurred

to me

that the

work of

harvesting

grapes

would

be so

demanding

Guy's lanky frame leapt from the truck bed. The wellingtons he had on his feet moved through the air and landed in the mud with a purposeful thump, firm in the brown loam of Fleurie, one of the most celebrated villages in the Beaujolais appellation, and where we were scheduled to harvest grapes that day. Guy scanned the vineyards that climbed the sides of the hunched mountains. I imagined that he focused his eyes on the far ends of the rows of vines, as though he could see the last grape on the last stem of the last plant.

To tell the truth, it had never occurred to me that the work of harvesting grapes would be so demanding. I'd worked my share of manual labour jobs so I figured bending over a row of vines and cutting off bunches of grapes wouldn't be so much of a strain. In fact, I'd had brief visions of singing my way through the vineyards, happily dropping clusters of fruit into a bucket, and finishing the day with a tipple of Beaujolais while sitting on a hillside as the temperate sun dropped below the horizon.

Now, five days into the harvest, the muscles in my back were on the verge of atrophying with the pain of eight-hour days bent down, grappling the bush vines and wrestling with the foliage. My fingers were scarred from missed swipes with the *secateurs* and scratches from rough

world

the deep

purple

globes

would

drop into

our pails

branches. My technique had been improving, though, and I could keep pace with most of the workers. Guy, however, stood in a league of his own.

A cry came from the foreman. We fifty or so pickers scattered to claim a row of vines we would clip the Gamay grapes from. The deep purple globes would drop into our pails which, when full, we'd hoist into the tubs carried by the porters who paraded the rows. The porters then carried the grapes back to the trailer.

Guy stationed himself two rows down from me. I could

see him, one knee at a right angle, the other following along the ground, his secateurs blurring through the leafy foliage of the vines. Clusters of grapes fell into his bucket like a shower of medallions.

Clouds drove in across the vineyards. They soon lay heavy above the green contours of the land. Then it started to rain.

We all ran down the hill, dropping our buckets and secateurs in the developing mud. We ran for the *camions* (trucks) where we knew our raingear was stowed. The château had given us olive-green plastic jackets and pants and we pulled these over our T-shirts and jeans. Then, looking much like a small militia camouflaged and lined up for something—if not entirely willing—we turned back to the vines, the rain now tapping on our backs and the sides of the hills.

But Guy did not don the green uniform. Instead, out of his duffel bag, dirty and torn from countless harvests, he pulled a blue plastic raincoat. The hood covered his cropped hair, and he fastened the zipper so the coat hugged his body. Besides the blue raincoat, the wellingtons on his feet were the only things that showed.

"Vite! Vite!" hollered the foreman, herding us back to our rows.

Guy bent over the grapevines and again I could see his hands tearing back the leaves, his clippers dissecting the vines. The overall motion was a fluid performance: fingers not missing a measure, secateurs aiming true. He sped along the row of vines, a rolled cigarette between his lips, smoke filtering out of his nostrils and wrapping around the grapevines.

And soon the wind picked up, lifting the leaves of the plants and whipping our raingear so it slapped around our

fingers

not

missing

a measure,

secateurs

aiming

true

bodies. The rain hit my back and legs and dripped into my shoes. It was a poor day for picking and morale was low. The vineyard was quiet.

Then I stood up momentarily, to stretch maybe, I can't recall, and caught a glimpse of Guy far off, where the vines ended. Gangly and tall, he dwarfed the vineyard, the big tarpaulin of a jacket fluttering behind him. The wind bucked it back from his rangy frame like a cape. Halfway up the hillside, he stood as though at the helm of a ship while we hunched over our rows, our backs green and humped like rolling waves.

Kuji

old school

Run DMC, Public Enemy, Grandmaster Flash and the Furious Five, the Sugarhill Gang. Old school. Public Enemy sought to fight the power and spread their social message, slandering political norms. Run DMC broke ground with unparalleled rhythms, rapping about style and the new cool. Grandmaster Flash showed his position with "White Lines" and "The Message." The early to mid-1980s were nothing less than the Rapper's Delight.

These pioneers laid the foundation for what came afterwards. Everyone from Snoop Doggy Dogg to Eminem has their roots well in the times of tracksuits and clamshell Adidas. These neophytes may have skills, but in one way or another they all reference back to the old school.

In much the same way, the Old World—Europe and the Mediterranean basin—signifies wine origin and foundation. The Old World developed theories behind wine, methodologies for wine, but most importantly, fostered credence in wine that the "new school" still gives props to.

public

enemy

sought

to fight

the power

and

spread

their

social

message

tradition

The Old World is the bearer of tradition. It prescribes the way wine has been made for centuries, using traditional methods and often questioning the modern science of winemaking. Most vineyard regions have been established for generations, with the same types of vines and the same philosophies towards growing, harvesting, and fermenting the grapes spanning the ages. Part of the philosophy embodies minimal intervention, particularly in the winery. The winemaker is seen as simply a hand that oversees the process from grape juice to wine, whereas the land, the vine, and the climate are the factors responsible for making a good wine.

Some would debate this. They would argue that we now have more knowledge about winemaking, and intervening techniques can work to turn what would be a mediocre wine into a noteworthy one. And some Old World winemakers are listening. They are the progressives, bucking the trend, taking wine in a new direction.

Is it for the better? Using technology to improve a wine, to make it softer, friendlier, easier to drink, cannot be a bad thing. Wine for the consumer, if you will. But would this put all wine on the same track? Wines, even though originating in different regions, would begin to assume homogeneity, possibly to the point where the regions were no longer distinguishable. In a William Gibson kind of way, we'd be moving towards a bleak future.

A compromise, perhaps?

terroir

One of those words with no direct translation into English, the French term "terroir" means the soil, the climate, and the topography of the vineyard. The concept of terroir also

using

technology

to improve

a wine,

to make

it softer,

friendlier,

easier to

drink,

cannot

be a

bad

thing

suggests the influential interaction of these three components, along with any others the surrounding environs may make on the site. It's a concept very close to home in the Old World.

So what, you may be asking, grows best in stony clay loam soils, with 500 mm (19.6 inches) of annual rainfall and a south-southeast exposure? While myriad studies have been devoted to finding the answer to this kind of question, and thus the scientific significance of terroir, the solution is never simple. Besides, there's nothing worse than standing in a room full of oenologists discussing dirt.

So we'd rather say: terroir is the soul of wine.

un example de terroir

We were visiting a château in Burgundy and, on an informal tour, followed the owner past presses and stainless steel vats, through musty *caves* lined with barrels full of wine, and finally upstairs to a room with a semi-circular window that overlooked the northwestern vineyards, the vineyards that produced the château's great white wine, Pouilly-Fuissé, from Chardonnay grapes.

It was overcast, grey, and we could see the two angular shapes of the mountains Vergisson and Solutré, and vineyards spreading up to the foot of them like a green sea lapping against two remote precipices. Our friend looked through the window and out at the vineyards. He was a tall man, and his habit of wearing a broad-brimmed hat made him seem all the more commanding.

"People from Canada and America visit me and they say, 'Let us try your Chardonnay,'" he said, gazing at his plants. "But they don't understand the meaning of terroir."

Then he suddenly turned around, looked at us intently, and explained as though he were talking for the generations of not only his château, but

un example de terroir *continued*

for all of France. "I don't make Chardonnay," he said, his voice almost a whisper, "I make Pouilly-Fuissé."

What he was explaining is, yes, the wine that he produces has come from a grape called Chardonnay. And 70 kilometres (43 miles) north, in the Côte de Beaune, wine is also made from the Chardonnay grape. But these two wines are dramatically different because of the different terroir, so much so that they require two completely different names. Names that are derived from the regions, and nothing to do with the grapes.

grapeWHERE

You're in a wineshop, standing in front of the ITALY section, but the label just isn't telling you anything. What happened to Chardonnay and Merlot? It's a long story, but in the meantime here's the lowdown on what goes into some of the common wines named by place.

grape	WHERE?
Cabernet Sauvignon, Merlot, Cabernet Franc	Bordeaux, FRANCE
Pinot Noir	Burgundy, FRANCE
Gamay	Beaujolais, FRANCE
Syrah	Hermitage, FRANCE
Syrah with a splash of Viognier	Côte Rôtie, FRANCE
Grenache, and 12 other grapes	Châteauneuf-du-Pape, FRANCE
Syrah, Grenache, Cinsault, Carignan	Côtes du Rhône, FRANCE
Carignan, Cinsault, Grenache, Mourvèdre, Syrah	Languedoc, FRANCE
Nebbiolo	Barolo, ITALY
Nebbiolo	Barbaresco, ITALY
Sangiovese	Chianti, ITALY
Tempranillo, Garnacha (Grenache)	Rioja, SPAIN

grape	WHERE?
Sémillon, Sauvignon Blanc, Muscadelle	Bordeaux, FRANCE
Chardonnay	Burgundy, FRANCE
Viognier	Condrieu, FRANCE
Chenin Blanc	Vouvray, FRANCE
Sauvignon Blanc	Sancerre, FRANCE
Sauvignon Blanc	Pouilly-Fumé, FRANCE
Touriga Nacional, plus others	Port, PORTUGAL
Chardonnay, Pinot Meunier, Pinot Noir	Champagne, FRANCE

france

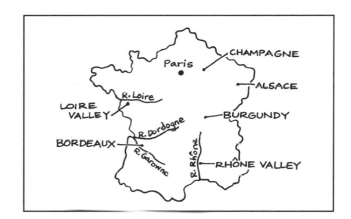

rules

Appellation Contrôlée (AC).

These wines have been made under traditional rules, and are usually the best quality as a result. The types of grapes, their origin, and the winemaking methods are regulated, and the region is printed on the label. Appears as "Appellation (region's name) Contrôlée" on the bottle, along with the name of the château or *domaine*, and the vintage. Think of AC laws as the governance of terroir.

VDQS.

Regulated regions waiting to be given AC status. This category makes up a mere one percent of all French wine.

Vin de Pays.

Fewer rules govern the "country wine." A wider range of grape varieties can be used, and the necessary quality of the fruit is not as high. Generally less celebrated, though a few pioneers have used the lax sanctions to make exceptional, well-priced wines. The grape variety can be published on the label, as well as the geographic origin.

Vin de Table.

"Table wine" with no declaration of geographic source, grape variety, or vintage. Very much the most basic wine, with quality akin to its stature.

wine regions

Bordeaux.

Arguably the most famous French wine, Bordeaux is like the wallflower at the high school dance. Pull him onto the dance floor too early, and he'll be stiff and apprehensive. Coax him out just at the right time and he'll show elegance and confidence up against his peers. But let him wait watching in the wings (for even up to 20 years!), and he'll astonish you with a grace and finesse that surpasses even the best Moonwalkers and Cabbage Patchers.

Burgundy.

If Bordeaux is the wallflower, then Burgundy is the DJ. Burgundy is either white (from the Chardonnay grape) or red (Pinot Noir), with both coming in a variety of styles.

if

bordeaux

is the

wallflower,

then

burgundy

is the

dj

And just as the best DJ can flawlessly switch between bossa and nova while still keeping the party hoppin', the best red Burgundies mix strawberry and cherry with an earthiness of truffles that defines one of the world's most celebrated wines.

Champagne.
Is there a better wine to open on your best friend's birthday, or at your brother's wedding, or to ring in the New Year? We (humbly) remind you that champagne is the most versatile wine for those times when you're serving particularly wine-unfriendly food.

Alsace.
Fine expressions of dry Riesling, Gewürztraminer, and Pinot Gris in the Old World, these Alsace whites have a hardy delicacy. An exception in the AC rule, these wines display the grape variety on the label.

Rhône Valley.
Stretching from the lower tip of Burgundy southwards towards the Mediterranean, the river Rhône snakes past the steep-sided hills where the sun ripens Syrah (in the north) and Grenache (in the south) to make some of the most powerful wines in the country. The powerhouse reds are matched only by the whites that will remind you, very brusquely, that the likes of Viognier, Marsanne, and Rousanne don't take it sitting down.

trends

Much of France is still trapped in tradition. In too many cases, they still make wines that rely on the reputation of the wine region such as Bordeaux or Burgundy rather than wines that can garner acclaim for their quality.

the best

red

burgundies

mix

strawberry

and cherry

with an

earthiness

of truffles

that

defines

one of

the world's

most

celebrated

wines

However, the past few years have been a wake-up call, as New World wineries have claimed more and more market share and, to the wine drinker's fortune, the French have heeded the warning bells. Quality is on the rise and so is innovation. Look for characterful wines from the more globally minded wineries.

italy

rules

Denominazione d'Origine Controllata (DOC).
Italy's version of the French AC system. There are hundreds of wines classified under the DOC legislation (usually labelled by region, again, not by grape variety), but the wine rules can be a bit lax at times. The government established the DOC about forty years ago to clean up their sprawling wine industry. We hate to think how much work this required.

DOCG.
This is DOC with an added G for *Garantita*. This "guaranteed" distinction was granted in the 1980s to the better wines within the basic classification, this higher tier being not so

much a carrot, but rather a christening of sorts. Altogether there are 13 of them.

Vino da Tavola.

The table wine of Italy was for the most part unremarkable until the 1970s and 1980s, when winemakers, fed up with the mediocrity encouraged by DOC rules, started making Vini da Tavola from unconventional grape varieties using contemporary techniques. This category soared and some table wine soon surpassed DOC in quality.

Indicazione Geografica Tipica (IGT).

So to gain some handle on this embarrassing situation that showed no signs of submission (and why should it, considering the calibre of these maverick wines), in 1992, the IGT classification was created for the modern-minded Cabs, Chards, Merlots, and Syrahs. More like a corollary of the DOC than another tier, IGT wines are more and more common today and their quality is just as diverse.

wine regions

Piemonte.

The home of Asti Spumante, the simply sweet, sparkling wine that's at the butt of too many "and when I woke up, I had a tattoo and I couldn't find my clothes" stories. But don't let this deter you from trying the aperitif or, for that matter, it's cousin, Moscato d'Asti. That said, the best wines of Piemonte (or Piedmont) are Barolo and Barbaresco. Both made from the black Nebbiolo grape, they can put even the best California Cabs in their place. Good wines from Barbera, too.

Veneto.

"In fair Verona, where we lay our scene" is the haven of

the

home

of asti

spumante,

the simply

sweet,

sparkling

wine

that's at

the butt

of too

many...

stories

Valpolicella Classico and its more robust relations, Recioto (sweet, with a bit of fizz) and Amarone (dry, upwards of 16% alcohol). The latter two are made from the higher quality grapes dried in lofts to make particularly potent wines. Soave is the white wine whose quality is banal in too many cases, though things are looking up.

Chianti.

We take it that a lot of Chianti was drunk in the 1970s so people could make candlesticks out of the wicker-cradled bottles that were synonymous with the wine. At least we can breathe some relief now that the reincarnation of lava lamps has petered out and Chianti is Chianti and not a candelabrum. The best expressions of Sangiovese, not only the grape responsible for Chianti but also the variety that dominates central Italy in any number of clonal variations, arguably comes from Chianti Classico Reserva and Brunello di Montalcino.

Super Tuscans.

Not a wine region, of course, and you won't see "Super Tuscan" on the bottle label. This is the nickname given to the radical wines containing Cabernet Sauvignon and Merlot that caused so much fuss in Italy some thirty years ago. Sassicaia is the most famous, with others falling under the IGT classification. All right, we admit the name sounds ridiculous, but how can you pass up a wine that is prefixed with the assertion "super"?

trends

For years Italian wines have suffered from large volumes of watered-down grapes. The market simply didn't demand a quality that tapped the country's potential. Mussolini didn't

a lot

of chianti

was

drunk

in the

1970s

so people

could

make

candlesticks

out of

the wicker-

cradled

bottles

help matters when he shut down wineshops and focused on producing grain instead of grapes. Maybe things would have been different if he'd seen French wine as the threat, rather than the Franc. Who knows?

Though it took a few more years than it might have, Italian wine is now at the forefront and just as good as its European Union counterparts. The Euro is the new Lira, and democracy the new dictatorship. But let's not get too far up the political creek. Fewer are the over-strapped vines that made nothing but uneventful dishwater and, from its varied climates and topographies, Italy is now making an impressive range of wines that stand up to the best of them.

Sicily is arguably the hottest wine region in Italy today. The Mediterranean island has a vast area for vineyard plantings, with a diverse landscape suitable for its native Nero d'Avola as well as lots of experimentation to grow the international varieties like Cabernet and Merlot. The bulk of these come under the IGT designation.

spain

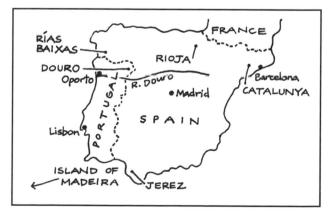

rules

Denominación de Origen (DO).

This sweeping classification that regulates Spain's grape growing, winemaking, and marketing has lost a bit of consequence with the proliferation of wine regions under the system. In short, with a whopping fifty-five regions sporting the DO tag, it's less and less of a significant stature. DO status can help along the quality levels of up-and-coming regions, but quirks in the system can stagnate established areas.

Denominación de Origen Calificada (DOCa).

Created to distinguish a level above the saturated DO. To date, only Rioja has been given DOCa status, but surely we'll see others.

Vino de la Tierra.

The equivalent of France's Vin de Pays. Country wine.

traditionally,

spain

releases

its red

wine

when

it's

ready

to

drink

Vino Comarcal.

Regional table wine.

Vino de Mesa.

Table wine.

Traditionally, Spain releases its red wine when it's ready to drink, rather than asking you to cellar it while it reaches its prime. An extension of this wine-world anomaly is the governance of ageing. Look for these on the wine label:

Crianza.

The wine has been in oak for at least six months (twelve months if the wine has come from Rioja or Ribera del Duero), with additional ageing to make up a two-year minimum.

Reserva.

Like Crianza, but in this case the wine has been in oak for

at least a year, in bottle (bottle-ageing) for at least a year, and aged at least three years in all.

Gran Reserva.
At least five years of ageing in total, with at least two in oak and at least three in bottle.

wine regions

Rioja.
There's always talk about wine regions in transition. It's a tireless topic in wine circles, whether the discussion is merited or not. Rioja, however, is worth talking about. The traditional Rioja style is a relatively pallid red, mostly from the Tempranillo grape, that has been aged in oak with the belief that more is better. American oak was the norm, and five years (Gran Reserva style) in barrel was commonplace. This makes a wine that is heavy with wood flavours and has tannins that'll glue your lips to your teeth. Years of further ageing in bottle were not only fancied, they were necessary to tone the wine into something drinkable. The best of these Riojas have a duality of elegance and power, an amazing combination if done right.

But things are changing in La Rioja. Some winemakers are electing to emphasize the fruitiness of Tempranillo with extended fermentation and more concise barrel ageing, often in the milder French oak, to make a wine that is friendlier from the start. This, undeniably, conforms to the modern wine recipe of bold fruit and softer, sweeter oak.

Ribera del Duero.
The origin of Spain's most distinguished (and pricy) wine, off in the no-man's-land of the Valladolid. Here, miles of brown chalky soil stretch, void of any digression in the

has

tannins

that'll

glue

your

lips to

your

teeth

form of mountain or otherwise. The sun bakes by day and the altitude makes for cool nights. Vega-Sicilia is the model of Spanish vinous success, a blend of Bordeaux's Cabernet Sauvignon, Merlot, and Malbec, with the regional Tinto Fino (AKA Tempranillo). Others have followed suit, though most prefer to stick with single-varietal Tinto Fino. Huge, powerful reds, deep in colour and fiercely robust.

Rías Baixas.
On the Atlantic coast, in the northwest. The area, riddled with fjords called *rías*, makes Spain's greatest white wine from the Albariño grape: dry, incredibly fruity, with a vibrancy best tasted when the wine is young.

Catalunya.
You don't need an excuse to open a bottle of fizz, it pairs perfectly with anything, and cava, the staple of Catalunya, costs a hell of a lot less than Champagne. As Stephen Merritt once crooned, "If there's a better reason to jump for joy, who cares."

On the other end of the price spectrum sit *Priorat wines*: red powerhouses from low-yielding Garnacha, Cariñena, and Cabernet that have stormed the world in the past twenty years. They're fantastically rare. And equally expensive.

Jerez.
The origin of Sherry, which comes dry (Fino) or sweet (Pedro Ximénez) or somewhere in between (Manzanilla, Amontillado, Oloroso, Cream). But to truly grasp the delicacy of Sherry, sample a Fino. The sharp, nutty flavour is a result of a *flor*, or yeast, that has created a film on top of the wine, inside the wood barrels. Then the contents of the barrels are blended in a *solera*, a matrix of vintages,

you

don't

need

an

excuse

to

open a

bottle

of fizz

to achieve the final wine. Best chilled, with a bowl of salted almonds.

trends
For Rioja, balancing between the older style that's heavily oaked and needing ageing versus the more modern, fruit-forward wines, the tendency is towards the consumer-friendly version of its Tempranillo. Fine for now, but we hope it doesn't mean the slippery slope of over-extracted flavours and bland, cookie-cutter wines made to please the masses.

Toro, on the other hand, just west of Ribera del Duero, is learning lots from its neighbour. With the potential for huge, high-alcohol, monstrous reds kept in check by an acidity made possible by the cool nights around the Duero, Toro is bringing its own Tinto Fino into the spotlight.

portugal

rules

Denominação de Origem Controlada (DOC).
The main quality designation for Portugal. DOC rules determine what types of grapes can be grown where, just like France's AC system.

Indicação de Proveniência Regulamentada (IPR).
IPR areas are those waiting for promotion to DOC status. Today there aren't many regions with the IPR tag, and the category will likely become extinct when the IPRs become DOCs.

Vinho Regional.
This is Portuguese country wine. With fewer controls on

grape growing and winemaking, wines within this designation are becoming more interesting.

Vinho de Mesa.
Table wine in its most basic form.

wine regions

Douro.

Alongside the world's greatest mysteries—ancient pyramids, crop circles, and Geddy Lee's unusually high voice—are the vineyards of the Douro. The area is named after the meandering river that runs from the Spanish border and spills into the Atlantic at the town of Oporto. But just why anyone would want to plant vines on riverbanks that, at some places, reach a perilous 60% grade and look as though they're going to slide into the water, is beyond us. Regardless, the grapes, particularly those from around Pinhão, combine to make Portugal's most esteemed wine: port. See Chapter 12: Bubbles & Brandy.

Madeira.

Another fine dessert wine from Portugal. The volcanic island of Madeira sits 640 km (397 miles) west of Morocco, planted out in the Atlantic. Its sheer cliffs, abundant rain, and lush greenery don't make it a likely candidate for growing wine-friendly grapes that only prosper in marginal soils and dry weather, but grapes will do the darndest things. Try this: soak a peeled and sectioned Mandarin orange in Madeira. Refrigerate. Serve over ice cream. Again, see Bubbles & Brandy.

trends

Since Portugal joined the European Union, it's been able to make good use of funding to improve its winemaking. With more resources in the vineyard, better technology in the winery, and, of course, marketing to woo us consumers, things are looking up.

As for the dessert wines, port prices keep rising and madeira is a rare sort of beast, so look for dry Portuguese wine if you want to keep on top of the trends and finish the day with some money left in your pocket. Some great reds are coming out of traditional port country, the Douro, and they're made from grapes that would normally have gone into the fortified wine. Instead of sending the fruit to its usual fate, a few visionaries are seeing alternate potential for the Douro.

Look for Alentejo wines as well. Lots of them from the Aragonês grape (the Portuguese name for Tempranillo), since the area borders Spain, and often bottled under "Vinho Regional Alentejano," outside of the DOC guidelines.

germany

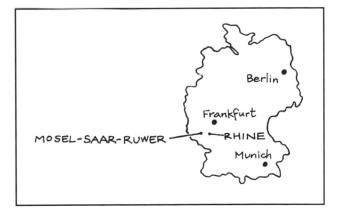

rules

German wine quality is based on the natural ripeness of the grapes. That is, by their methodology, the riper the grapes, the better the wine. Whether you agree with this or not is one thing, but with a climate like Germany's (where even getting the grapes to ripen is an annual challenge), it kind of makes sense. You know the saying about sour grapes.

QmP (or Qualitätswein mit Prädikat).
Wines are made from the ripest grapes. The best of these are examples of elegant balance between sugar and acidity, the former being the aspiration, the latter the inevitability. Within QmP, the following will appear on the label, from less to more sweet, where the sweeter the wine, the more esteemed it is: Kabinett, Spätlese, Auslese, Beerenauslese (BA), Eiswein, Trockenbeerenauslese (TBA).

QbA (or Qualitätswein bestimmter Anbaugebiete).
Given to wines that don't have the ripeness to make QmP. You don't have to try too hard to get a QbA designation.

Landwein.
Wine of the land? Germany's stab at France's Vin de Pays.

Tafelwein.
The most basic of German wines.

wine regions

Mosel-Saar-Ruwer.
The rivers Saar and Ruwer join the Mosel that runs into the Rhine. By far the best wines here are made from Riesling grown on mineral-rich slopes where Mosels have an elegance that isn't mirrored by the more robust Saar-Ruwer wines. On flatter land, Müller-Thurgau is grown, though it makes a fairly drab white.

Rhine.
Composed of the Nahe, the Rheingau, the Rheinhessen,

where

even

getting

the

grapes

to ripen

is an

annual

challenge

and the Pfalz. Again, Riesling leads the quality spectrum, which is as broad as anywhere else in Germany. The best wines range from racy refinement to rich and full bodied, while the worst are simple mouthwash.

trends

the best

wines

range

from

racy

refinement

to rich

and full

bodied,

while

the worst

are

simple

mouthwash

Though Germany is capable of producing some of the best expressions of Riesling in the world, particularly in off-dry versions, its wine laws are intolerably confusing for the consumer and allow for overproduced, poor quality wines.

Labelling has much to do with this. Germany's top vineyard names can be used, in part, for wines that come from the general vicinity, though they may have nothing to do, quality-wise, with their namesake.

This shortsighted marketing coup has run its course. The wines have lost much respect, and for newer consumers, it's simply easier to avoid the cryptic German labels and go browsing in the Aussie wines or somewhere where the bottles say "Riesling" and be done with it.

But as Germany sees this, they're turning up the quality on their better wines. We hope their wine laws will get sorted out. Meanwhile, start to recognize the nomenclature and pick out the better Rieslings. For starters, find a QmP Riesling with a Kabinett or a Spätlese designation. The Kabinett will be a less sweet, less complex wine with a good apple/lime character, whereas the Spätlese will be honeyed and will have a plush feel in your mouth. They'll both be excellent examples of off-dry whites.

eastern europe

Vines have been planted in Eastern Europe for centuries, though it is only now that we're seeing some selection in our wineshops. In addition to the indigenous grape varieties, there have also been more recent plantings of the Cabs and Chards.

Hungary.
The end of Communism meant the end of heavy government subsidy. Competing in the free market, many of the big wineries have gone bankrupt, though there's been a resurgence of smaller, quality-oriented winemakers. The best wine out of Hungary is a dessert wine, called Tokaji Aszú, made from Furmint and Hárslevelü grapes. A description of Tokaji is in Bubbles & Brandy.

Bulgaria.
An exporting giant relative to the rest of Eastern Europe, with nearly 90% of its production made for export, Bulgaria is gaining increasing importance in North American and British markets. The country has focused on Cabernet, Merlot, and Chardonnay (and the wines are labelled as

vines

have

been

planted

in eastern

europe

for

centuries

174

such), a good reason why the wines go over well in other countries. On top of this, they've put together sophisticated wine laws. Look for Controliran (like French AC) and Reserve (oak aged) wines.

Greece.

Upon joining the EU, Greece beefed up its wine exports, though it's predominantly the larger companies that have been able to showcase their wines, particularly those in the oft-sought "international" style. However, much Grecian wine remains traditional, the obvious example being Retsina. This wine, that likely needs some getting used to, has pine resin added to it.

the new
world

There I was, frantically grasping for words, standing at the pay phone in the lobby of a youth hostel in Santiago, Chile. Lord knows I was concentrating, trying hard to ask questions and jot down directions. There was mention of a certain-numbered bus, followed by instructions to transfer to another, smaller bus. One thing was certain, my Spanish ability had been humbled; without contextual gestures and body language, I was reduced to bumbling.

I had come to South America in search of the grape. It was a pilgrimage to the land whose wines had helped me through late-night sessions of university papers and exam studying. Chilean wine had offered salvation on a student's budget. The phone conversation was an attempt to arrange a trip to visit a winery in the Panquehue area of the Aconcagua Valley, a famed region north of Santiago. Two English ladies I met while in Buenos Aires had put me in touch with a friend of a relative, who in turn was to arrange a meeting for me with the winemaker.

Directions concluded, I had confidence enough to muster "*muchas gracias*" and hang up. Then I proceeded to do what any male with an inkling they'll get lost should do: I politely asked the women to accompany me. Not only could they ask directions, their Spanish was better.

The buses in Chile are grand, replete with flamboyant

i had

come

to

south

america

in

search

of the

grape

world

paint

schemes

that would

put the

flames on

a firebird

to shame

paint schemes that would put the flames on a Firebird to shame. And there's bingo on the long-haul routes. We left Santiago in comfort, heading through the mountains that ring the Chilean capital. The first leg of our trip took just over an hour, more or less northward. As we travelled, the smog dissipated, uncovering clear views of the newly snow-topped Andes to the east. Our directions—reinterpreted after another phone call—told us to get off the first bus in some small dusty town, then transfer to the number 28. This crossroads was not exactly bustling, but the locals

and their chickens were friendly. With half an hour to spare, we picked up a few fresh-fried cheese empanadas and Fanta Naranjas.

The next bus would more appropriately be called a shuttle, with a 20-or-so passenger capacity. We loaded up and rolled out. The late February sun created a perfect T-shirt temperature. The driver said he'd call out our stop, which was 25 minutes away. Hills all around, the vines soon came into view, prime grape-growing country.

Not knowing exactly what to expect, I had worn my brown cords and collared shirt, the most formal outfit in my backpack. We disembarked at the winery's driveway and made our appearance. Quite honestly, it's a good thing I went accompanied. The owner was looking forward to seeing a distant relative, and any friends of hers must be, in the least, tolerable. In fact, it soon became apparent we were in for a treat, as lunch was being prepared and three generations of this wine family were in attendance.

After introductions and kisses on the cheeks, we were led on a complete tour of the winery. Thirty-five acres of Sauvignon Blanc and Cabernet Sauvignon grapes, in manicured rows abutting the hills. Next we walked through the production facility, where old oak *barriques* were counterbalanced by new stainless steel tanks. As the proprietor continued his talk, my mind went through Spanish calisthenics, leaving me aching for nourishment.

It soon came with the call for lunch, so we headed to the main residence for some patio dining. Across covered walkways and through brilliant patches of green grass we trotted, the whole scene altogether dreamlike. What, did I just see a happy child rolling in the grass with a Golden Retriever pup?

my mind

went

through

spanish

calisthenics,

leaving

me

aching

for

nourishment

the

sauvignon

blanc

went

well

with the

chicken,

but the

same

cannot

be said

for

pinochet

and sorbet

The family was generous, the conversation convivial, and the food simply delicious. The estate-grown Cabernet Sauvignon and Sauvignon Blanc were served with a green salad, juicy fried chicken, and hand-cut chips. Questions of my life in Canada were asked, stories of the winery's traditions were told, and then dessert arrived at the table.

The dessert itself was great, freshly made sherbet and ice cream from down the road, but with the sweets came a bitter topping of politics—call it a case of bad timing, an issue of misunderstanding, or simply the legacy of Pinochet. As mentioned before, I was visiting the villa with two English women. It so happened that the infamous (or revered, depending on how much land you owned) ex-Chilean leader General Augusto Pinochet had recently had troubles in Europe. Specifically, in 1998 he was put under house arrest in England, pending talks of a trial to determine his role in past human-rights abuses against the Chilean people.

Our hosts thought this had been preposterous. My friends were guilty by national association. As a guest, I reserved my right to keep my mouth shut. The Sauvignon Blanc went well with the chicken, but the same cannot be said for Pinochet and sorbet.

To be fair, in the end a stalemate was reached, and the visit was none the worse. Personally, I left with a better appreciation of the history of Chilean wine, a couple of bottles, and the reminder that grapes and politics don't always pair.

new school

If the Old World is a story of terroir, then the New World is one of science — analog making way for digital. The results are debatable, depending on tastes and sensibilities. While some revere vinyl for the subtle pops and cracks of its warm, imperfect sound, others appreciate the crystal-clear clarity of compact disc.

The designation of "New World" refers to those areas outside of Europe and the Mediterranean basin. *Vitis vinifera* spread around the world on the backs of European explorers and missionaries, an intruder in the name of sanctity. These first grape growing experiments were met with varied success. The conquistadores had no problems producing wine in South America, but British colonists could only scratch their heads as native *vitis labrusca* vines flourished along the Eastern Seaboard, while their imported specimens faltered. From these humble beginnings no one could have foreseen the impact the New World would come to have upon the world of wine.

fruit-driven

It is telling that no New World language has an equivalent for the French word terroir. One simply hasn't been necessary. For the traditional Old World, the grape is a product of the land, while in the New World, the grape is the product itself. We buy Sauvignon Blanc instead of Pouilly-Fumé.

The New World generally does not have to contend with tradition, which admittedly can be stifling, even in its best intents. Here, growing the best grapes is often a tale of human vs. nature, or at least working with nature to secure favourable results. Thus, technology is judiciously employed when it makes sense. Regulation in the New World is handled differently too. Quality is not enforced by stringent codes or laws, but rather afforded by the other arbiter of regulation—the invisible hand of the marketplace.

consumer-friendly _____

The wine business is, despite all its romantic intentions, still business, and is therefore subject to the same laws of the marketplace:
"Know how to make a small fortune in the wine business?"
"Start with a large one."

So goes the old joke, and the bottom line is no laughing matter. This makes the case for efficiency, and where efficiency treads, technology follows. The New World created the push for technology in the vineyard and winery, from drip irrigation to mechanical harvesters, straight on through to temperature-controlled, stainless steel fermentation tanks. Innovation is a way of life in the New World.

As much as technology lends efficiency to the wine-making process, the bottle still has to be sold. Hence the New World holds dear the needs of the consumer. The rise and subsequent dominance of varietal wines, wines produced predominantly from a single type of grape, is no accident. After extensive marketing and education, the average consumer has expressed an understanding and appreciation of naming wine by the grape. Chardonnay, Merlot, Shiraz, and Cabernet Sauvignon have become the purebreds of the grape world, with a modern indifference to mutts. When was the last time you saw a cockapoo at the dog-park?

Of course, with such a market-driven philosophy rises the notion of fashion and consumer whims, reflected in the uprooting of unfashionable vines. The whole scene has been known to rile the sensibilities of Old World producers, but to be fair, the Old World is a place where wine is indoctrinated in culture. This is not so in the New World.

trends

Still, if things were simply black and white, Old and New, the world of wine wouldn't be nearly so much fun. Sooner or later all things come around, and many in the New World are seeking to establish tradition, or have begun applying Old World techniques in their high-tech wineries. Now there is talk of barrel fermenting, blending, and even the idea of, gasp, terroir. Fears are being voiced that the New World is in danger of producing an intercontinental wine that is homogenous and bland, much in the style of processed global pop culture. But fear not, sales of vinyl are on the rise, and even some CDs these days incorporate samples of old records, scratches and all.

canada

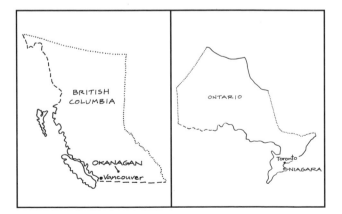

Canada has a long history of homegrown wine, dating back to the early 19th century. Granted, most of it has been the calibre of plonk. Wine production didn't really get serious in Canada until NAFTA crashed the party, but recently Canucks have been proving their wines are worthy. Icewine seems to be Canada's trump card, but don't overlook interesting whites and reds that have been ripening well in some of Canada's not-so-freakish hot spots (including obscure hybrid varieties like Marechal Foch, Baco Noir, and Vidal).

wine regions

Niagara.
Hugging the shores of Lakes Erie and Ontario in the province of Ontario, Niagara has seen large investment in vineyards and wineries. Riesling, Chardonnay, and other white varieties have proved most successful, with diehards insisting they can craft some big reds. Icewine is also big in these parts, and is beginning to spread its viscous cheer around the world.

Okanagan.
Over on Canada's west coast, in the province of British Columbia, the Okanagan Valley is quickly solidifying its role in Canadian viticulture. Lesser-known white varieties such as Ehrenfelser and Bacchus do well, along with the usual cast of green skins. Reds can also ripen in this certifiable Canadian desert.

trends

The Canadian reputation for being nice and gentle bodes well for wine. Overall, Canadian producers use a less-is-more approach, employing hands-off winemaking techniques and embracing more natural grape growing practices. In the west keep an eye out for wines from the Gulf Islands and the Fraser Valley. Back east, watch for Niagara fighting to remain dominant and the emergence of Prince Edward County. Wines are also made in the provinces of Quebec and Nova Scotia, but good luck finding them outside provincial lines.

california

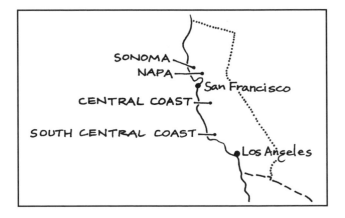

Quite simply, Cali put the New World on the wine map. California, in the 1960s and 1970s, proved to the world that fine wine did not only come from France, a feat that subsequently changed the face of wine dramatically. California continues to influence, from garage winemaking to cult wines to industry-leading concepts in wine tourism. Throw the dubs up for the West Coast.

wine regions

Mention of California brings dreams of sunshine, endless summers, and the Beach Boys. While the entire state is essentially one grape growing greenhouse, the high quality juice is generally sourced from pockets closer to the coast.

Napa.

The most famous region, recognized early (late 19th century) for its grape growing potential. Today, after bouts of phylloxera, Prohibition, and skyrocketing prices, everybody and everybody's lawyer would like a piece of Napa. Postcard beautiful and with the crowds to prove it, Napa isn't afraid to state its fine wine claim, manifested in bold wines of various types. The warmer valley and hillsides of northern Napa are known for reds such as Zinfandel, Cabernet Sauvignon, and Merlot, while cooler patches to the south do well with Chardonnay and Pinot Noir.

Sonoma.

Abutting Napa to the west, Sonoma is still on occasion misrepresented as Napa's country-bumpkin cousin. While the roads may not be as jammed (Sonoma's yet to see regular weekend gridlock *à la* Napa's Highway 29), the area is anything but rustic. Closer to the coast, with fog and Pacific breezes rolling in, Sonoma wines tend toward finesse before they slap you in the face with huge fruit. Sonoma is well suited to producing an array of wines, with no shortage of treats made from Pinot Noir, Chard, and old vine Zinfandel.

Central and South Central Coast.

Across the Bay and south of San Francisco starts the region generically known as the Central Coast. Wine drinkers in the know are flocking to these wines, and for good reason. If you were to head from San Fran to L.A.— taking the scenic route—you'd come across a variety of wineries in differing mesoclimates around Santa Cruz and

everybody

and

everybody's

lawyer

would

like a

piece of

napa

Monterey. Further south, around Paso Robles and Santa Barbara, lie Santa Maria Valley, Santa Ynez, and Santa Rita Hills. Damn fine wines, if a little hard to find.

trends

While hipsters deplore "over-oaked Cali Chards" and turn their palates to wine from other regions, California continues to offer exciting bottles of various kinds. True, some Cali wineries have lost touch with their soaring prices. However, there's no need to fight your way onto mailing lists or pay exorbitant fees for the latest cult wine to enjoy California. Look for second labels, a winery's offshoot label, coming out of Napa and Sonoma, seek out values from the Central Coast, and if you really want to be adventurous, try wines from the lesser known Sierra Foothills and Temecula regions.

other states

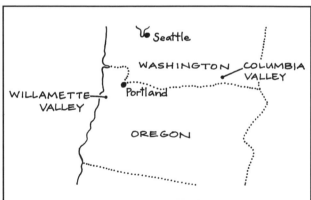

It should be noted that 48 of the 50 states grow grapes and make wine. Of course, it should also be countered that the amount of wine produced in 47 of these states together amounts to a mere trickle of California's production. Still, in the interest of fairness, and always cheering for the underdog, it's important to acknowledge achievements.

wine regions

Washington.

Washington wines continue to garner attention. Most grapes are farmed in the southeastern corner of the state—a dry, desert-like anomaly protected from the abundant coastal rains by the Cascade Mountains. Columbia Valley is the main area, with the subregions of Yakima and Walla Walla gaining attention. All kinds of whites are made, and reds ripen as well, with Washington winemakers crafting some great Riesling, Merlot, and Syrah, to name but a few.

Oregon.

Prone to wetness, finicky, and with hippy tendencies, Oregon has the attitude and, arguably, the climate for that artsy-fartsy grape—Pinot Noir. Some call Oregon the Burgundy of North America, and besides the aforementioned Pinot Noir you'll find great Chardonnay, as well as Pinot Gris. Overall, Oregon has characterful wines, made in relatively small production, that are hard to find outside the state.

New York.

The state of New York has a long history of grape growing, most of it native labrusca vines or hardy hybrids. However, as knowledge and technology improve (and romantic notions of winery ownership endure), serious attempts to make premium wine are being undertaken. The passion is evident, though again the wines are not easily accessible outside the general vicinity.

trends

States with established industries will continue to learn about their climates and unique geographies, and wines will improve in kind. Mavericks will start new wineries in obscure locales, and while not all will work, some interesting results may find their way onto local shelves. Wineries in Idaho are going strong, and even Texas is in the wine game. Don't mess with the U.S.

chile

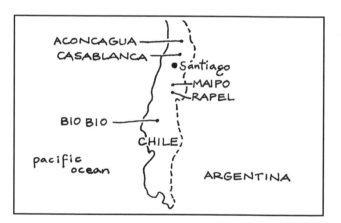

"Phylloxera free and proud!" would be a true if somewhat unappetizing slogan for Chile. This long, skinny thing of a country is in many ways a grape-growing paradise. Chile's natural barricades (Andes to the east, Pacific to the west, desert to the north, and Antarctic hinterlands to the south) kept the phylloxera aphid at bay while it ravaged vines throughout the rest of the world, affording Chilean vines the chance to continue growing on their own rootstock.

Add oodles of sunshine, good day-to-night temperature fluctuations, and great soil sites, and you have happy grapes. Chile literally burst onto the world wine scene in the 1980s with rich, ripe red wines. Acknowledged value and aggressive export campaigns have ensured shelf space in stores around the globe, and continued investment will no doubt keep it so.

wine regions

Aconcagua and Casablanca.
A short ride north of Santiago lie many of Chile's most acclaimed vineyards. Many wineries call the Aconcagua Valley home, while a bit further west, the cooler Casablanca Valley receives ocean breezes that lend a helping hand to stellar whites made from Chardonnay and Sauvignon Blanc.

Maipo.
Literally starting in the suburbs of Santiago, the Maipo is the northern section of Chile's Central Valley, the real mother lode of Chilean grape production. If you buy a Chilean wine, odds are the grapes were grown in the Central Valley. Merlot and Cabernet Sauvignon can't get enough of Maipo's warm surroundings, and they develop into ripe fruit bombs.

Rapel.
As Chile's cities recede, the grapevines of the southern Central Valley take control. Grapes of all kinds as far as the eye can see, from vitis vinifera destined for a bottle to plump, seedless grapes that will end up on your table.

Bío Bío.
The vines stretch south all the way to the Bío Bío River, some 400 km (248 miles) from Santiago. Still far from the polar

cap, the region's cooler climate nevertheless makes for more appropriate white grape growing. As rising real estate prices and concessions to urban sprawl encourage exploration of new vineyard sites, we'll likely see more wines from this southern area.

trends

While Chile began ditching its "cheap wine" banner a while ago, budget-minded wine drinkers can take heart, as Chile will continue to produce solid-value bottles. That said, however, the rising tide of outside funding (mostly from France and California) signals a trend towards higher-end things to come. Expect Chilean wines to become more elegant, with the finesse of fine wine. For some fun, seek out the variety Carmenère, which these days is pretty well unique to Chile, and can make some stunning, inky, spicy reds.

argentina

Across the Andes lies the other South American wine-producing powerhouse of Argentina. The sensual land of *tango*, *gauchos*, and *asado* happens to make vast quantities of wine (at last count Argentina was the fifth largest producer in the world), which until recent times was quaffed almost exclusively by thirsty locals. However, changes in domestic consumption and neighbouring Chile's worldwide wine success have altered things, to the good fortune of imbibers around the globe. Most of Argentina's vineyards are in the foothills of the Andes, at relatively high elevations, irrigated via canals expertly devised by the Incas thousands of years back.

wine regions

Salta.

Argentina's highest and most northern wine region, known for fresh whites, with potential for slow-ripening reds with cool character. The Cafayate Valley is Salta's best-known district, with claims of some of the world's highest vineyards, hovering at 2000 metres (6500 feet) above sea level.

Mendoza.

Unquestionably the heartland of Argentina's wine production. Just south of the picturesque city of Mendoza (itself resplendent with a latticework of canals) are Luján de Cuyo and Maipú, home to most of Argentina's largest *bodegas* and wine companies. Malbec and Cab Sauv brood in these parts, basking in the potent sunshine.

Río Negro.

Following the Andes south will lead you to Río Negro, an area on the cusp of Patagonia. Lots of topography is devoted to vine, though relatively few wines from this southern section are currently seen abroad.

_____

Argentina is a sentimental place, and the best Argentine wines echo this moodiness—a combination of stubbornness, creativity, and sensuality—that permeates the culture. Just look at the grapes that seem to thrive in Argentina. In red there's juicy, earthy Malbec that is dark and intriguing in the glass. Torrontés is a white that, at its best, is an exotic mix of spice and perfume that will get you in the mood. And given Argentina's wine tradition, diligence, and desire to export, there's no doubt that Argentine wines will continue to make inroads.

south africa

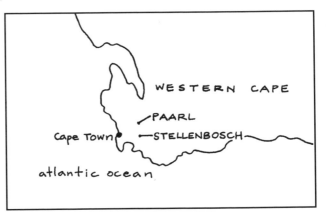

On the whole, South Africa is a curious wine region. It has a long history of winemaking, though it's not Old World. Then again, the typical South African wines aren't exactly molded in the fruit-forward style of their New World compatriots. Middle World? Regardless, the industry was stunted as a result of apartheid, so no doubt the potential for South African wines on an international scale will soon show itself. Already, versatile offerings, from ripe reds to cooler climate whites, are being stocked. Also, don't overlook South Africa's unique Pinotage, a dark horse of a grape, from a crossing of Pinot Noir and Cinsault, that can be downright funky when done right—the perfect wine to take aboard the Parliament mothership.

wine regions

Stellenbosch.
For all intents, Stellenbosch is South Africa's most important wine region. Tonnes of Shiraz, Cabernet Sauvignon, and Merlot are planted here, though whites have been known to fare well too.

Paarl.
An ad hoc region with confusing boundaries, drawn more in accordance with politics than with geographic considerations. As a result, the soils and climates of Paarl vary, the grapes grown differ dramatically, and the subsequent wines wear a variety of stripes.

trends

The Huguenots passed their winemaking skills on to the Dutch in the 17th century, and now the old stalwarts in South Africa should do the same to the new group of winemakers. They should then be humble and allow these modern vintners to do their thing, so that South African wines can be permitted to find a solid identity. Then the message in the bottle will be brought to the world.

australia

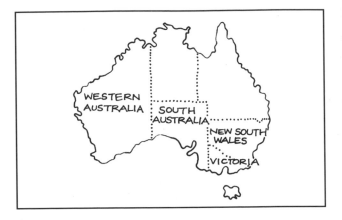

The big kid on the New World block, Australia is omni-present in the wine world. To some Australia's a bully, to others a worthy leader, but regardless, it's undeniable that Australia is shaking things up. Their wine styles suit many a modern drinker, their marketing speaks to the consumer, and bottles from Oz continue to fly off the shelves. With the obvious dedication to technology and vineyard invest-ment, Australia is clearly intent on maintaining a leading role. If you were to pick an all-star Australian wine line-up, it'd read Riesling, Semillon, and Shiraz, with Cab Sauv, Merlot, and Chard coming off the bench. Oh yeah, Shiraz is Australian for Syrah.

wine regions

New South Wales.
On Australia's eastern shore, the state of New South Wales is home to a bevy of well-known wine regions. The growing conditions can be hot and muggy, less than ideal, but proximity to Sydney (and potential for wine country

tourism) no doubt helps stoke the winemaking fire. It's in New South Wales that you'll find the Hunter Valley, capable of glorious wines, including the mysterious Semillon that seems to magically transform with time in the bottle. Other districts of note include Mudgee, Orange, and Hilltops. Finally, further inland lies the irrigated badlands of Riverina, with a legacy of keeping the thirst of the masses quenched.

Victoria.

Starting from the coastal hub of Melbourne, the wine areas of Victoria more or less spread out fanlike. Overall cooler climates can produce wines with finesse, though just when you think all is serene, a walloping Victoria Shiraz will come along and put you in your place. Murray Darling, Pyrenees, Yarra Valley—these are some of the famous place names, areas that churn out many a wine of character. Victoria also produces fine stickies (sweeter dessert-style wines) from Tokay to fortified Muscats, notably from the area of Rutherglen.

South Australia.

For many, the wines of South Australia are synonymous with Australian wines—period. The majority of Australian wine is produced here, and all the mega-Aussie wine con-glomcrates are either based in, or have significant interest in, these parts. Much of South Australia is downright hot, ripening grapes to the brink. Subsequently these get turned into the fruit-forward wines that are now all the rage. This is the land of the Clare Valley, Barossa, and McLaren Vale.

Across the hills, the East Barossa Ranges introduce a cooling influence as evidenced in stellar Rieslings from the Eden Valley. Further south, far down the coast from Adelaide, we find the Limestone Coast zone, home to Padthaway, Coonawarra and the like, making expressive wines of cooler disposition.

Western Australia.
Crossing vast swaths of open plain and vinous emptiness, you'd be forgiven for thinking Australia goes on till the end of the world. Until finally, finally you see mirage-like bodies of water, which turn out to be the junction of the Southern and Indian Oceans. This is where you'll find many of Western Australia's vineyards. Here, there is a long history of winemaking, though current favour is to focus on the wines of Margaret River and the Great Southern subregions.

trends

Will Australia dominate the future wine world? Will all wines soon taste Australian? Maybe not, but there's no denying the obvious influence. Australian wine companies have quickly become some of the world's largest, and Australian winemakers continue to fly around the world and lend a consulting hand. Good wines, in both value and premium categories, will continue to come from Down Under. Undoubtedly, some terrible, gimmicky wines will also find their way across the seas. All in all, Australia's passion for the vine and commitment to technology will quicken the pace of change in the wine world.

new zealand

Across the Tasman Sea from Australia, New Zealand has quickly been developing a solid reputation. The geography is different and so are the wines, with cooler climates lending a distinct freshness. Think New Zealand and most likely Sauvignon Blanc will come to mind. "Bracing," "pungent," and "pure," are words used to describe unique Kiwi Sauvignon Blanc, and it's only slightly extravagant to say that this wine has captivated the world.

wine regions

Hawkes Bay.
On New Zealand's North Island, Hawkes Bay has a rep for being the country's red wine region. So, given the dominance of New Zealand's whites, it's not surprising the region is lesser known. With a climate that is warm rather than hot, plantings of Cabernet Sauvignon, Merlot, Pinot Noir, and Cabernet Franc are *de rigeur.*

Marlborough.
On the northern edge of South Island awaits Marlborough,

home to famed Marlborough Sauvignon Blanc. The fame comes from a pure and tangy expression of the grape.

trends

Not content to be seen as one-dimensional, New Zealand has been concentrating on producing tasty reds. Pinot Noir is a logical candidate, with hopes of another Kiwi star to follow in Sauvignon Blanc's footsteps. Chardonnay also shows well. Perhaps Merlot and Cabernet Franc will shine—though the jury is still out. Overall, the wines of New Zealand should continue to offer a unique and desirable style.

wine in asia?

Sure, and we're not talking saké (rice wine) or *umeshu* (plum wine), but wine wine, from the grapes we all know and love.

Japan. Japan not only consumes a lot of wine, it also produces it—mostly in Yamanashi Prefecture, a relatively short train ride west of Tokyo. Of course, Japanese law permits imported grapes to be mixed with domestic produce. "Real" Japanese wine exists, albeit in limited (and expensive) quantities.

China. Widely planted with vines, though most of the grapes end up on the kitchen table. However, there is much hope for China's wine future, not the least of which is motivated by outside interest. It's inevitable.

Thailand. Some wine lovers, or more accurately dreamers, have attempted growing quality wine grapes in Thailand, but results have thus far been unmemorable. Given the tropical climate this isn't altogether unsurprising. Thanks, but we'll reach for the mangosteins and rambutans. Still, hopeless romantics ourselves, we give an "A" for effort and remain open to future offerings.

India. Again, lots of vineyards, though the majority of these grapes are not used for wine. Undoubtedly, given time some fearless entrepreneur will come along, raze a little hell, and plant significant amounts of vitis vinifera.

bubbles & brandy

chapter twelve

bubbles

tossing

back

bowls of

bourbon

and

laughing,

exhaling

through

yellow

teeth

It was April, yet the way the wind whipped off the bay it felt like November. Gulls dipped and dove in the gale and squawked loudly. The sky was a terrible steely mix of grays and I turned up my collar and tightened my jacket. Tires rumbled over the broken pavement, bounced in and out of potholes, and clapped against streetcar rails. I crossed the road to a hotel that was covered in gold. The doorman was also covered in gold and he pulled open the heavy door when I got too close.

"Good day," he smiled with a golden smile.

"Yes," I said.

"Are you here for the wine tasting?"

"Yes."

The lobby of the hotel was stuffy, the stale air infused with cigar smoke. I passed a dozen men lounging in leather armchairs, letting the ash of their cigars fall on the carpet, tossing back bowls of bourbon and laughing, exhaling through yellow teeth.

I pushed open a set of doors and suddenly I was standing in the middle of the wine tasting. The room was gymnasium-sized, the ceiling reaching an extravagant height with dark curtains draped down from it, hugging the walls. I pictured dusty angels flying along the rafters, blowing on broken trumpets.

& brandy

"Toot," said one.

"Toot toot," said another.

The crowd melded around me as I walked forward, the loose dresses of the women and sweaty jowls of the men stirring the room. The women and the men opened their mouths and lifted their wineglasses in raucous delight. My head spinning, I struggled to a booth that was serving port and stood between damp bodies. The man serving wine was tall, with wild hair straying from his head. We talked.

sweaty

jowls

of the

men

"Just wonderful!" he said in a slanted accentuation. (He was not a local.)

"What?" I asked.

He reached behind the table and brought forth a small green bottle with a tiny cork that made a slight sound when it came free of the neck. Gold fluid fell into my glass, coating the sides with a viscous thickness.

"It's a sixthee-three."

"1963?" I squinted in the fluorescent blaze radiating from the ceiling and stuck my nose into the wineglass to find a wall of crushed elderflowers and caramel candy, reeking of years.

"Oh no, 1863." The words floated from his mouth.

Then the bottle was gone and in its place were the loose dresses and sweaty jowls. I was lost in the crowd as it wavered back and forth and launched me across the floor.

"1863," I heard the crowd mumble.

And suddenly the crowd was not a wine tasting crowd but one of men moving barrels, pushing equipment across a dirt floor, and yelling loudly over the industrial din. Sunlight passed through windows set high up on monstrous walls. It smelled like brandy and wood. Then they were yelling at me, as all I could do was stand clutching the glass of port.

"Mmm?" I asked. There was wine in my mouth.

An angel flew past me—dropping from the vaulted ceiling—looking like it might crash into a stack of barrels, only to recover at last. Out the open door it careened, a syrup dripping from the bell of its trumpet. It parted into the open sky, flew in a loop and brought the brass mouthpiece to its golden lips in ceremony. The trumpet didn't work because it was filled with elderflowers and caramel.

I managed to regain my composure and when my head

"it's a

sixthee-

three"

204

stopped spinning I was back in the wine tasting. Most of the crowd had dissipated outdoors to the taxi queue and an usher was saying something to me that I couldn't make out. The nectar of the port was still on my tongue. My disbelief that a wine could survive a century and a half was slowly coming undone.

Kuji

alternative wines

While there is certainly a wine for every occasion, some occasions may call for a wine other than the usual red, white, or pink. Sure, there's nothing wrong with popping the cork on a meaty California Cabernet Sauvignon when the birthday cake is being served, and there's no harm in sipping a zingy Sauvignon Blanc from New Zealand on a winter evening while you're curled up on the couch reading the latest Douglas Coupland book. But if you find the angel food cake gets drowned in the sandpaper tannins of the Cab, and sharp flavours of gooseberries don't do much to ward off a wintry chill, why not try some alternatives?

bigger bottles

(Kenji had a dream once that he was at a party on a cruise ship, surrounded by women. One of them revealed an oversized bottle of champagne. Veuve Clicquot, he claims to remember. He also swears that the bottle was a Jeroboam, the largest bottle of champagne he's ever drunk from, in reality or in delusion.)

Depending on size, champagne bottles have different names:

size	name
750 mL	Bottle
1.5 L	Magnum
3 L	Jeroboam
4.5 L	Rehoboam
6 L	Methuselah
9 L	Salmanazar
12 L	Balthazar
15 L	Nebuchadnezzar

champagne

Champagne is synonymous with celebration. When the neon ball in the Big Apple makes its descent every December 31st, all over the city bottles of champagne are queued with anticipation. When Puff Daddy leans over his birthday cake to blow out the candles every fourth of November, DMX and Ludakris are waiting patiently to open the bottle of Cristal.

And though the literary leaders of our day enjoy the sparkling wine from the Champagne region of France, champagne was first made popular by the scholarly London café society in the 17th century. In fact, until then, the preferred beverage from Champagne, led by the monk Dom Pérignon, was not sparkling, and the accidental carbonation of the wine caused endless problems due to the weak glass bottles of the time. The development of stronger bottles helped, but even so, every year a good half of the production would break from the internal pressure.

The pressure is a result of a second fermentation of the wine that happens inside the bottle, after the cork has been set in place. With yeast cells still kicking around in the wine, and with a bit of leftover sugars, fermentation will re-start and the trapped carbon dioxide (a product of the fermentation process, see Chapter 9: Winemaking) will give wine its fizz.

Once the winemakers in Champagne were able to understand the second fermentation process, and control it by getting the amounts of yeast and sugar just right, they could begin to make the wine bubbly without risking catastrophic explosion.

Champagne is made from three grape varieties: Pinot Noir, Pinot Meunier, and Chardonnay. As a classic example of making white wine from black grapes, the black Pinot Noir and Meunier grapes are pressed, without their skins included in the mix, keeping the juice, and ultimately the wine, clear.

Champagne producers will each have their house wine. The house champagne is non-vintage, or NV for short, and there will not be a specific year printed on the label. This means that, rather than the wine having been made from grapes of a single year, many vintages were blended together—10–50% of *vins de réserve*, the reserve of previous years that has been stored in vats at the winery. The blending allows the winemaker to reproduce the same-tasting champagne every year, and this is what is commonly sold in stores.

champagne

is made

from

three

grape

varieties:

pinot

noir,

pinot

meunier,

and

chardonnay

Vintage champagne, made from a single year that has been particularly good, is also produced, though it is more expensive and generally has more body than its NV counterpart. A rudimentary grasp of French will clue you in to the other types of champagne: Blanc de Blancs, from only Chardonnay; and Blanc de Noirs, from the two black grapes of the region. Pink champagne has usually had red wine added to it, though in rare cases the skins of the black grapes are used to give it its colour.

But do remember, the next time you're on the invite list to P. Diddy's birthday bash, make sure you dress appropriately (Sean John, please) and make sure there's a bottle of *prestige cuvée*, the luxury version of a champagne firm's NV house blend, under your arm. Möet & Chandon makes the legendary Dom Pérignon and Roederer makes, you guessed it, Cristal.

how sweet it is

A sweetener, or *dosage*, may be added to the champagne before it leaves the winery. This level of sweetness should be shown on the label.

Brut (dry, with no dosage)
Sec (just off-dry)
Demi-sec (medium-dry)
Doux (medium-sweet)

Beware: the addition of the dosage may be a veil to hide a poor-quality wine!

other sparklers

Although sparkling wine does not all come from the Champagne region in France, recent lobbying by the producers of the well-known bubbly made sure that their wine was the only wine that could bear the name "champagne."

Other sparklers have to have other titles. Crémant is sparkling wine from areas of France other than Champagne and, just as its origin is varied, its flavour can be all over the map. Cava is almost exclusively from the Catalunya region of Spain, around Barcelona. It is somewhat less refined than champagne, so expect a more rough 'n' ready style. Italian Spumante, long associated with easy drinking, is a sweet, simple sparkling wine that's refreshing, if nothing else. Prosecco is a bubbly from Italy, with more character than its cousin of less repute. Sekt is Germany's answer to sparkling wine, though for a long time the undemanding market didn't do much for the general quality of the wine. Recent progress, particularly using the Riesling grape, has improved its image and Sekt can have as good acidity and finesse as its better counterparts.

These and other sparkling wines from Australia and California, whose quality can differ enormously in the absence of traditional rules, are made on the same principles as champagne and are often more affordable. The better bubblies have been made by the champagne process, and will sometimes read *méthode traditionnelle*, or equivalent, on the label. The lesser ones have simply been injected with gas, a system that is commonly known as the bicycle-pump method, though the *méthode bicyclette* is not talked about that much.

producers

of the

well-known

bubbly

made sure

that their

wine was

the only

wine that

could bear

the name

"champagne"

sparkling cocktails

Kir Royale
Champagne with a dollop of cassis. To really impress your date, start the evening with this aperitif.

Champagne Mojito
Champagne with fresh mint, squeezed lime juice, and sugar. The first time we came across it, we were in a designer bar in London where the food was haphazard and the vibe was trendy but cautious.

Mimosa
Champagne and orange juice. If you go to James' grandparents' house on any given Sunday, you will stumble into Sunday Morning Church Service. Dixieland on the stereo and mimosas all around.

port

after

generation x

comes

generation y.

after shampoo

comes

conditioner.

and after

dinner

comes

port

Things are getting a little out of hand these days. Reality TV shows, flared jeans, junk e-mail, and GMO produce. They defy our good sense, and we are never safe from being blindsided by the next trend. We hesitate to change the channel on the television, and brace ourselves before we open the newspaper every morning. We feel ill at ease walking the streets of downtown, not knowing what fad will come from around the next corner.

Okay, it may not be that bad, but it is comforting to know that some things still remain logical. So as you settle down to the latest bestseller, just remember: after Generation X comes Generation Y. After shampoo comes conditioner. And after dinner comes port.

Port has its roots in the 17th century when trade conflicts between England and France forced the English to source their wines from elsewhere. They found a steady supply in Portugal and to ensure delivery of a quality product, added brandy to the red wine to kill any leftover yeast that could ruin it on its way north. Of course, this produced a slightly sweetened, high-alcohol wine that would later be called port, after Oporto, the city from where it was shipped.

These days, the brandy is added at an earlier stage, when the fermentation of the wine is not complete and there are still some sugars left from the grape juice. The alcohol of the brandy kills the active yeasts and fermentation ceases. What is left is a wine with residual sugar and about 18 to 20 percent alcohol: a perfect wine to end the evening. Serve with cheese or dark chocolate.

types of port

Ruby: the most basic of port styles and also the most affordable. It's been aged for only a few years, so it retains a deep ruby colour. It has a strong flavour, with intense fruitiness at best, but a pungent stewed taste when mediocre.

Tawny (or Aged Tawny): aged in wood for such duration that the colour has been all but extracted, leaving behind a pale orange—or tawny— coloured wine. The bottle will indicate the age, or average age, of the wine, such as 10, 20, or 30 years. Good tawny comes with delicate flavours of fruit and caramel, and can have a unique nutty character.

Vintage: the most celebrated of all the port styles, it is made from a single vintage, and even then only in the best years. The wine is aged for two or three years, then bottled and sold. After that, it needs up to 30 years, or sometimes longer, to develop. Remember, patience is a virtue.

Late Bottled Vintage (or LBV): is also from a single year, but spends more time in wood (four to six years) so it does not need the extensive bottle ageing that vintage port does. Ready to drink from the time you buy it, at best it is a deep purple colour with a rich, voluptuous character and distinct fruitiness.

madeira

Madeira is another fortified wine, but certainly the only one that required (historically) a round-trip sea voyage to mature properly. From the Portuguese island of Madeira, the wine was loaded onto ships heading to India and by the time it had crossed back and forth over the equator, it had cooked to a nutty, often smoky, flavour. Depending on the style, it can range from dry with lofty acidity to a caramel sweetness.

These days, however, not many frigates of the Dutch East India Company sail the high seas, so *estufas* have taken the place of ship's hulls for places to mature madeira. (Estufas are rooms or tanks that store the wine and can be heated to replicate the ocean crossing.) The result of this harsh technique is a wine that is so robust, even after you've opened the bottle it can survive ad infinitum. The advantage of this, of course, is you can always have a bottle on the kitchen counter for adding extra flavour to your cooking, then for a glass later on.

sherry

the

temptation

of

stereotyping

the

sherry

drinker

Unlike port, sherry does not reap a great deal of attention in North America. And the typified sherry drinker who persistently comes to mind is the notoriously flamboyant uncle from the movie *Withnail and I*. But we'd be falling prey to the temptation of stereotyping the sherry drinker as the old, stuffy bourgeois of rotund design and shifty, black peppercorn eyes, as was dear Uncle Monty.

Where, in fact, sherry is a tremendously underrated aperitif, ideal for whetting the appetite before dinner. Styles of the Spanish wine range from the dry Fino and Amontillado to the sweeter Cream sherry, the former two being generally more appealing with a clean, almond-like nuttiness, best served chilled.

vermouth

Vermouth is a wine fortified with grape spirit and flavoured with herbs, and proof that even the cool martini crowd has to pay homage to wine. Of course, its intention may be lost in the Cran-tini, the Saké-tini, and other hip variations on the theme, but nevertheless, Mr. Bond, for one, would accept no substitute.

Vermouth also comes in red, a sweeter version of Italian origin that's often drunk on the rocks with a twist of lemon. The French equivalent is a golden hue and drier. The beauty of vermouth, however, is its mundane beginnings. It serves as a sponge for the infinite lake of mediocre wine that pools in France and Italy, being made from simple table wine not suitable for the grocery store shelves.

when martinis go out of style

This martini craze seems to be rolling on longer than the high-protein, low-carb fad. And certainly longer than wearing a necktie over a T-shirt. But all good things must come to an end, so what do you do when you're left holding the (dry) vermouth?

The Dry Manhattan
- 2 oz whiskey
- 1/2 oz dry vermouth
- A dash of Angostura Bitters (optional)
Mix over ice, strain, serve with a twist of lemon peel.

The Gin Fizz
• $1/2$ oz gin
• $1/2$ oz dry vermouth
• Juice of half a lime
• 2 oz dry white wine
Mix with ice in a tall glass, then add soda to top up.

The Devil's Cocktail
• $1 1/2$ oz dry vermouth
• $1 1/2$ oz port
• $1/2$ tsp. lemon juice
Stir with ice, strain.

El Presidente
• $1 1/2$ oz white rum
• $3/4$ oz dry vermouth
• Splash of red curaçao
Mix. Serve.

noble rot

there is

poetic

contradiction

in a

burly

man

There is poetic contradiction in a burly man, his face contorted in concentration, sipping Sauternes (the pre-eminent sweet late harvest wine from the Bordeaux region of France) from one of those delicate tulip-shaped dessert-wine glasses. It's always a refreshing scene at an otherwise oppressively predictable wine tasting.

So go ahead and hit the gym, toss the pigskin, grunt loudly, but don't forget to sip the syrupy wine that is a miraculous result of a curious mould called *botrytis cinerea*, or known by its more attractive nickname, "noble rot." The mould grows on the grapes during the damp evenings, causing the fruit to lose water, which concentrates the sugars of the juice within the berries.

From these intensely flavoured grapes comes a sweet wine that, at its best, is rich and golden with a floral perfume, like velvet in your mouth. Less successful years, however, when weather conditions have not been favourable to the fungus, create wines that are much more basic.

Other countries are also able to make wines from botrytis-affected grapes, provided they have the uncommon climate necessary.

tokaji aszú

Without question, Tokaji Aszú is Hungary's flagship wine. Again botrytis cinerea plays an instrumental role in shrivelling the grapes, particularly the Furmint grape, to a point where they look anything but appetizing. The fruit that is not transformed by the rot is made into regular wine. Then, the clusters of affected grapes, called Aszú, are pressed into a sweet paste and added to this wine.

When you see a bottle of Tokaji Aszú, notice the number of *puttonyos* that have gone into the wine. Aszú paste is measured in puttonyos—the more the merrier (and the sweeter). This wine has a luscious flavour of fruit and chocolate, and adopts an almond-like taste with age. The Esszencia mark on the label indicates an even more intense version.

late harvest

Though not as storied as the wines from nobly rotted grapes, late harvest wines are nothing to turn your nose up at. As the name implies, these wines are made from fruit that has been picked towards the end of the harvest, and as a result come from grapes that are riper and have more concentrated juice.

late

harvest

wines

are

nothing

to turn

your

nose

up at

Good late harvest wine can be full of character, exploding with flavours of apples and pears, cantaloupes and honey. Poorer examples are merely syrupy and sickly sweet.

icewine

Possibly ranking in the top four most likely souvenirs from Canada (beside maple syrup, smoked salmon, and hockey), icewine is quickly becoming a national institution. Though it was originally made in the Mosel in Germany as *eiswein*, icewine has found its home in both the Niagara region of Ontario and the Okanagan of British Columbia.

The grapes are left on the vines until they freeze in the impending winter, and only then are they picked, with true, patriot love. When pressing the grapes, as the water within the fruit has frozen, only the juice containing the sugars is drawn out, yielding a very small quantity of concentrated liquid.

Reports of bootleg icewine being made in China out of frozen table grapes faltered the market a few years back, confirming a need for icewine police. The situation has stabilized, though we're sure you can still find the odd bottle being sold alongside the Rolex watches and Burberry handbags.

possibly

ranking

in the

top four

most

likely

souvenirs

from

canada

enjoying
wine
chapter thirteen

enjoying

the

perfect

example

of simple

spontaneity

is the

impromptu

picnic

Perhaps the perfect example of simple spontaneity is the impromptu picnic. It does not require pretense—it can be a familial outing, a friendly get-together, even a romantic interlude. It does not require much planning—though co-operating weather, an open space, and a long, free block of time are advisable. Most importantly, it does not require much prep. Bravo to those who take the time to prepare a proper menu and pack it away in an appropriate basket. However, that is a planned picnic, a worthy endeavour unto itself, but of a completely different genre. The impromptu picnic seizes the day, makes an opportunity out of a moment, and at its best reaches into the soul to dish up transcendence. Without a doubt, an impromptu picnic is one of my preferred ways to enjoy my wine.

California is prime picnic territory, with a near guarantee of sunshine, bountiful wine and produce, and a varying topography that offers infinite vistas. I personally enjoy picnicking near the beach, where the whiffs of salt air and crashes of waves upon the shore create a natural ambience and act as mood enhancers, if you're not picnicking with your mom.

Once I drove with my mother from Los Angeles to visit my brother in Santa Cruz. A lazy Saturday afternoon, perfect spring sunshine, and a desire to catch up with each

wine

other proved motivation enough for an impromptu picnic. There was a winery nearby that I wanted to visit, so the three of us made haste for the Santa Cruz Mountains, with a quick pit stop for some food.

Not much is needed for an impromptu picnic. Since it was the weekend and farmers' markets were open, we stopped and perused the local goods. A loaf of bread is necessary for starch and sustenance, be it baguette or Winnipeg rye. Cheese is a natural accompaniment, and two kinds are always better than one. Olives are a personal

be it

baguette

or

winnipeg

rye

favourite, with pits please! Fruit always refreshes; it makes sense to bring whatever's in season. Of course, chocolate is compact and travels well, a simple but tough-to-beat dessert. We bagged our groceries and headed for the hills, to a quiet spot we had been tipped off about, next to a rambling stream. The views went on for miles. Miles and miles. Along the way, we stopped at the winery, tasted some great bottles, and decided a Muscat would pair with our picnic lunch.

The food and wine were taken care of, but when we arrived and unloaded, I realized I had forgotten to bring glasses. I had my corkscrew and pocketknife, but no glasses. If I had been solo I probably would have resorted to sipping from the bottle, but with my mom in attendance, a classier strategy was required. It was then that I spotted some empty plastic water bottles lolling about the back-seat. A quick cut later and we had appropriate drinking vessels, two per bottle. The upside-down top, complete with cap, suits traditionalists with its pseudo-wineglass-shape, while the bottom offers up superior stability. The glasses worked great, the food was delicious, and the afternoon passed with nary a care.

like your wine

It's one thing to know wine; it's altogether a better thing to enjoy wine. Let's be firm on this: there's no point in drinking the stuff, even in moderation, if you don't enjoy it. Just as there's no point in being in a relationship for comfort's sake. Playas we're not, so we cannot purport to be experts in the relationship game, but it seems to us that compared to the complexity of companionship, wine should be a simple thing to enjoy. That said, we're not playa hatas either, and in this age of prefabricated lifestyles and shifted responsibilities, we recognize that a little handholding can be provocatively comforting. Thus, we offer some tried-and-true ways to enjoy wine.

attend a wine tasting

Attending a wine tasting is a great way to get intimate with a good variety of wines. Tastings come in an array of formats and styles, and trying many wines in one sitting permits a comparative evaluation not possible in a typical evening of wine drinking. We've been to regional tastings, country tastings, varietal tastings, gala tastings, new product salons, blind tastings, etc. Regardless of scheme, it's beneficial to head into a tasting with a strategy, lest you be overwhelmed both by the wine and the crowd.

the arrival

It's helpful to know the format of the tasting before you go. Some tastings err on the side of fancy, and while we've never been turned away from the door in our jeans, know that you will draw attention if you show up in your civvies. Arrive punctually or fashionably late, but do afford the wine fair accord and give yourself enough time to do the rounds.

the entrance

Once past the gate and coat check, enter with eyes wide open. The first order of business is to find a wineglass, and unless this is a sit-down affair, there should be a table piled high with crystal (well OK, it's probably glass). Then, upon entering the tasting room, give it a good once-over, suss out the scene, breathe in the vapours. It's time to determine a tasting strategy.

tasting strategies

Classic.

The classic approach would be to work your way through the wines in ascending order, from bubbly to whites to reds, then on to sweeter desserts. Getting more technical, within each category you can progressively work through each wine type as well. For example, when tasting whites, taste lighter to heavier, from Sauvignon Blanc to Riesling to Chardonnay. Tasting wines in this manner helps to avoid overwhelming your palate. Trying a huge, tannic red would essentially deaden your senses to a lighter, more delicate, white.

Niche.

There's also the potential for palate fatigue. Larger tastings may have 50, 100, or even more wines to try. With such a selection, at times it may be advisable to concentrate on a specific wine type or country. Be disciplined, focus on a niche, and the odds are the next day you'll better remember the wines you tasted.

Give 'er.

Of course, who are we to judge? If it's your thing, just give 'er and taste any of the wines in any order.

the exit

As the tasting continues, you will probably notice the note-taking getting sloppy, the grins becoming wider, and the stares lingering longer. These are the people that have been swallowing, not spitting. It's at this point that we usually employ our exit strategy, making a quick escape. It can be a jungle out there.

wine tasting tips

Start with bubbly.
When available, we always start with the tiny bubbles. Not only does this lend us a slight air of class, it also serves to refresh the palate. For this reason, sparkling wine can also be a good transition taste, between white and red, red and dessert, etc.

Hit the bread/crackers early and often.
Even if you taste and spit, your body will absorb some alcohol. Bread and crackers will not only keep you on the level, they will also help cleanse your palate for the next wine taste.

Remember the water.
Just because it's a wine tasting, it doesn't mean you can't drink water. Don't forget, alcohol dehydrates, water hydrates. Walk the middle path to better find your nirvana.

Return to your favourite.
It's always nice to end a tasting with a final sip of the wine that most wowed you.

Don't give out your number.
It's up to you, but don't say we didn't warn you.

brown baggin' it

If you don't feel like heading out to a tasting, you can always bring one home. Holding a wine tasting in the comfort of your own space, with a few friends, is easily one of the best ways to enjoy wine. Not only is it cost efficient, but a casual environment, with people you trust, can work wonders in soliciting honest opinions about the wines. There's a bunch of "home tasting kits in a box" on retailer's shelves, but all you really need is a modicum of ingenuity and some common sense. Here's how we've successfully pulled off home tastings:

Figure out who's coming.
Eight to twelve people is manageable. Anything more and you may as well have a party, not a tasting. Anything less and there may not be enough wines to try.

Choose a theme.
Will you be tasting wines from a specific region? Of a certain grape? The same type of wine from different countries? For all intents, the possibilities are endless.

Choose a host.
If the host agrees to prepare some food, then the guests can bring the wine. Usually, one bottle per guest or couple will suffice.

Get together on the agreed upon date.

Prepare wines.
It's enjoyable and advisable to taste the wines blind—that is, without knowing which is which. Not surprisingly, labels and price points can have a dramatic effect on opinion. Those little brown paper bags do a fine job of concealing the bottle, and they have the wonderful side perk of looking oh-so-urban. Have one person put the bottles in the bags (some tape around the neck will hold the bags in place), have another mix up the order of the bottles a bit—heck, have a third open the bottles. All in the name of proper scientific method.

Taste the wines.
A fun way to do this is one at a time, so you and your friends can discuss the wines at length. For even more craziness, name each wine after someone in attendance

who's
coming?

what's the
theme?

who's the
host?

when?

which
wines?

(the paper bag works as a canvas too). You'll be surprised at how creative the comments on the wine can become— "Anna's a little funky" or "Billy is smooth but has a short finish!"

Compare.
After the wines have been tasted, go back and polish off the bottles, choosing favourites, etc. If so inclined, it's beneficial to take notes; it will aid your memory of wines tasted.

making wine

Making your own wine is so retro cool it should be illegal. (At least it was pretty cool making wine on the down low during Prohibition.) If you're serious about wine (or if you're on a serious budget), making your own makes a lot of sense. You'll not only gain a more complete understanding of the winemaking process, you'll get to drink the fruits of your labour. Plus, for couples, with all those siphons, buckets, and hydrometers, winemaking is the new potting wheel. Just ask Patrick Swayze. Only remember that proper winemaking requires good hygiene.

go to a u-brew _____

This is the easiest way to make your own wine. It also works well if you don't have space at home. Really, who makes wine in their bathtub these days? Real simple: you head to a U-Brew (results vary, we recommend you find a shop with a good rep), choose a wine, sprinkle some yeast to get the party started, and go on your merry way. Then return at the allotted time and bottle your bounty.

the wine kits

If you're the hands-on type, you can buy a winemaking kit and get to work in the privacy of your own home. Kits typically come in four- to eight-week incarnations, in just about every wine style. The key is the concentrate, or lack thereof. Some kits come with more juice concentrate, like a vacuum-packed version of a frozen can of OJ. Others use more *juice* juice, so you don't add as much water. We've had better results with the juicier kits. You'll need to invest in some equipment, but it's a minimal outlay, and not complicated.

wine from grapes

To keep it real, like the Italian and Eastern European immigrants, you'll have to make wine from grapes (for a great wine scene head down to Little Italy during each harvest and watch the diehards buy their grapes and exchange winemaking gossip). Granted, if you take it to this level, you're making a real commitment. You'll need lots of equipment, lots of effort, and lots of patience. It's hardcore, but it will prove fulfilling, and as an added bonus, this approach allows you to stomp grapes with your bare feet.

visits to wine regions

Coincidentally, grapes are grown (and wine is made) in some of the most beautiful areas of the world. For those with antsy feet, this is not an unhappy occurrence. Everyone seems to enjoy a trip to wine country, and why not, when you can capture first-hand the essence of the vineyard, gain some insight into wineries, and taste some treats? There's not really a bad time to visit a wine region, each season offering its own nuances, but keep in mind that harvest time can be chaotic for the wineries, and not conducive to casual visits.

Most wine regions have clued in to the possibilities of wine tourism, making it pretty easy for you to navigate your way around any given area. That said, grape growing is farming, meaning many wineries are only accessible by personal transport. Plans of "finding" yourself in Europe through a glass of wine and a Eurail Pass are not that feasible. As a final consideration, note that not all wineries appreciate visitors, so if there isn't a sign announcing they're open to the public, you'd best be on your way. Happy touring!

the *HALFAGLASS* top five wine region visits

(This list is made in no particular order and with the caveat that many of the world's wine regions await exploration. In other words, it is a constant work in progress.)

Burgundy, France
The Côte d'Or is one of the world's famed wine regions. It is also fairly easy to bike around, with kind slopes and small towns dotting the landscape. This is the place to make a Pinot Noir pilgrimage. Start in Beaune, fuel up on *escargots*, and pedal to your heart's content.

Mendoza, Argentina
Mendoza is not only a pleasant place to spend some time, the vineyards surrounding the city are superb. Plus, it's one of the few regions where it's easy to take a local bus to some of the wineries, which always adds colour to an adventure.

Clare Valley, Australia
South Australia is the heartland of the Aussie wine industry, and thankfully much of it is accessible from Adelaide. In particular, a great day trip is the Clare Valley. From the city, head north in the morning and tour the wineries dotting the rolling hills. Be sure to pick up a couple of bottles of

famed, screwcap Clare Riesling, then head back to Adelaide for dinner at one of the numerous BYO Asian restaurants along Gouger Street.

Piedmont, Italy
Piedmont doesn't really need an introduction, and if you go in October and have a bottle of aged Barolo in La Morra accompanied by a pasta dish topped with fresh shaved white truffles, well, that doesn't need an explanation either. Heaven on Earth.

California, USA
Napa and Sonoma are swell, but we're talking the Santa Maria Valley, further south, with a unique east–west disposition that opens right onto the Pacific. It's a cooler climate, not as crowded as its brethren to the north, and the wines are darn tasty.